Dark Woods, Chill Waters

Ghost Tales From Down East Maine

Dark Woods, Chill Waters

Ghost Tales From Down East Maine

Marcus LiBrizzi

Down East Books

Camden, Maine

Cover photograph © Doug Landreth/Corbis

ISBN 978-0-89272-752-0

Printed at Versa Press, Inc., East Peoria, Illinois

6 5 4 3 2 1

Down East Books
Camden, Maine
A division of Down East Enterprise, Inc.
Book orders: 800.685.7962
www.downeast.com
Distributed to the trade by National Book Network

Library of Congress Cataloging-in-Publication Data:
LiBrizzi, Marcus A., 1964-
Dark woods, chill waters : ghost tales from Down East Maine / Marcus
LiBrizzi.
p. cm.
Includes bibliographical references.
ISBN 978-0-89272-752-0 (trade pbk. : alk. paper)
1. Ghost stories, American--Maine. I. Title.
PS648.G48.L53 2007
813'.6--dc22
2007019394

TABLE OF CONTENTS

Down East Maine—A World Apart

Brooding over the ghost tales collected here is a sense of unspeakable horror and malice. A faceless figure in black materializes to collect the soul of a dying man. A skeleton rises to greet the corpse of her sister. Footsteps echo in secret rooms and hidden passageways. Bloodstains reappear mysteriously at the scene of a crime. Searching for his next victim, a wrathful specter stalks Jasper Beach. In an old portrait, the face of a woman undergoes a sudden change, grimacing in rage. Then there is the gory spirit of a murdered peddler who can be summoned at will, and the phantom light that pursues a man in a Native American tale. Standing at the side of the road, the apparition of a headless woman places a curse on a lone motorist speeding away in terror through Black's Woods.

It is likely that you will never encounter ghost stories more horrifying than those contained in this book. They all originate from the most remote, hence mysterious, section of the eastern seaboard, sometimes called the "lost coastline" or the "lost Down East." Primarily comprised of Washington County in the state of Maine, this is the region's last untouched piece of shoreline, positioned—and often forgotten—between Bar Harbor and Campobello Island, New Brunswick. Down East Maine is a region rich in both scenic beauty and supernatural lore.

Certainly, the landscape lends itself to the ghost story. Although people refer to Washington County as the "Sunrise County," there is a certain irony to this name. Jutting out into the Atlantic Ocean, this rocky, easternmost edge of the United States is always the first piece of the nation that is shrouded in the darkness of night. Thus, it is the land of the sunset. Then, of course, there is the sheer gothic beauty of the Bold Coast; its granite cliffs thundering with crashing surf captivate the imagination. And within the sudden fogs that roll in from the sea and in the ever-present miles of dark forest, there lurks the sense of the unknown, that deepest source of human fear. In stark isolation stand the small coastal villages separated by a maze of inlets and peninsulas and vast tidal marshes.

History hangs heavy over the land, in part because it was settled so long ago. Native Americans have occupied the region for thousands of years. Europeans explored and created outposts here long before the Pilgrims established the Plymouth Colony. The result is a set of deep traditions involving the invisible world. With the economic decline that took place in the region after the Civil War, these ghostly traditions flourished. The air of a ghost town hangs over many communities, as seen in their abandoned farms, decaying mansions, empty wharves, and family burial plots swallowed by the forest. Going Down East is, truly, like going back in time.

Among the dread phantoms haunting the pages of this book, I'll leave it for you to decide which is the most frightening. Undoubtedly, it will be one of the legendary ghosts with the capacity to cause harm or even death. The cast of characters includes a cannibal ghost with a heart of ice that cannot be melted, the apparition of a murdered man who comes in with the fog to seek vengeance, and the phantom of a dead shipmaster who returned from the grave and claimed the life of his widow. Dreadful, indeed, is the baby-killing specter from Dennysville, and deeply disturbing is a pack of spirits or demons who took the shapes of a young man's family in order to lure him into the woods.

As a university professor, I've researched ghost stories from all over the world, and I can honestly say that nowhere have I found accounts as frightening as those uncovered from the lost coastline of Maine. In some of the college courses I've taught, I have assigned students to gather tales of the supernatural from local residents. I am indebted to those students and residents; without them this book could not have been written. Ghost stories are essentially collective in nature, involving unique histories, interlocking lives, personal experiences, and generations of storytelling.

As a whole, the tales brought together here weave the darkest of tapestries, its vision or design exceeding the worst of nightmares. Therefore, brace yourself for an experience not soon forgotten.

I

The Headless Specter Of Black's Woods

No other place in Maine is as shrouded in legend as the Black's Woods Road. This short stretch of Route 182—between the towns of Franklin and Cherryfield—presents travelers with some of the most beautiful country Down East. The area is mountainous, with views of foliage and crags of rock above and shimmering bodies of water in distant valleys below. The road winds around part of Fox Pond, then climbs to the top of a small mountain, aptly named Catherine's Hill.

The subject of the Black's Woods legends is the specter of a young woman who was decapitated and who stalks the road, sometimes headless, sometimes not. As the story goes, anyone seeing the spirit of Catherine must stop and offer her a ride. Woe to those who don't, for the phantom will curse then, and soon afterward they will die.

One version of the legend involves a salesman who was traveling at night through Black's Woods when he saw the headless ghost hitchhiking. In terror, the man sped past the figure, but his relief at getting away was short-lived; when he looked in his rearview mirror, he saw the phantom sitting in his back seat. Through panic and, perhaps, a weak heart, the man crashed his car and became another victim of the specter.

The stories of Catherine's demise take many forms, but the outcome is the same—a ghostly hitchhiker in a flowing dress who most often appears on foggy nights, usually around Catherine's Hill, but sometimes near Fox Pond. The most common account is that Catherine and her boyfriend were traveling back from a prom in the 1970s when their car hit a tree, killing both of them. Catherine was beheaded as she went through the windshield, and the young man disappeared, in all accounts his body never found. As a result of her accident, the ghost of Catherine stalks the road, searching for her head, for her boyfriend, or maybe just trying to get home.

Variants of Catherine's death are essentially the same, except the time period may be the 1960s or the 1950s. One account of the story is set in the 1920s, during Prohibition, when wealthy flatlanders traveled to the Down East region for drinking parties and hunting expeditions at a nearby lodge. Catherine, a young servant at the lodge, was taking a break and riding in a Model T Ford with a male companion. Coming around the road near Fox Pond, the man lost control of the car, which swerved over the embankment and crashed into the water, beheading Catherine. Of interest is the fact that there is still a perfectly preserved Model T Ford at the bottom of Fox Pond, as numerous divers have testified. In the story's earliest version, set in the nineteenth century, Catherine died in Black's Woods on her wedding night. As she and her groom traveled by stagecoach toward Cherryfield, a strange ground fog crept around them. When they reached the top of the mountain that now bears her name, something spooked the horses, and the coach rushed out of control, crashing into a tree at the bottom of the hill.

Catherine was beheaded, and the rest is history.

What do we make of such bewildering variations? They are, in a real sense, the creepiest part of the legends. It is eerie how the stories get cast back farther and farther in time, as if the tales of Catherine are historically changing attempts to make sense of a presence that is far older and far more mysterious than any specific account could indicate.

One wonders what the Native Americans thought of the region. In Passamaquoddy lore there are many stories of lake monsters and malignant spirits: Perhaps the legends of Catherine are different ways of understanding the same phenomenon experienced for centuries in the woods around Fox Pond.

Local resident Matt Leighton may have put to rest the story of Catherine. He owns land that contains the grave of a certain Catherine Downing, who died December 29, 1862. According to Matt, the legends of Catherine blow out of proportion an event in which Miss Downing, then a young woman, left a social gathering early one evening. While she was traveling home, it began to grow dark, and fearing she would lose her way, she sat by the road to rest until dawn. Meanwhile, her alarmed family searched for her. She was found the next morning, alive and completely intact, if not a little tired and stiff. While Matt's theory is interesting, it does not explain the specific sightings by so many people from different walks of life, including individuals who are new to the area and who have never heard of the headless woman of Black's Woods. Witnesses to the phantom are literally so numerous they could fill a book. But let the following accounts convince you that there is something out there in Black's Woods.

Debora Newell encountered the specter when she first moved to

Maine. She had heard the rumors, but she didn't give them any credence. Then late one night, while driving back from Bangor with some friends, she saw something she'll never forget. She writes, "There were patches of mist around the roads on the sides, in the trees. It seemed like all of a sudden there was a patch in front of me, and I didn't give it any second thoughts. But as I got closer to the mist, it seemed like it was starting to take the form of a woman, with her hair flowing behind her and in a long white gown and a shawl on her shoulders." Debora put on the brakes, thinking she was going to hit an actual woman on the road, but the car went through the figure, which dissolved into mist.

An even more baffling incident was recounted to me by Dennis Boyd. He heard the story from a woman, since deceased, whom we'll call Abby. It occurred when she was a child. One cold and rainy day she came down with a bad throat infection and had to travel to Franklin to see the doctor. Her father, a lobster fisherman from Steuben, drove her there. As she and her father were coming up Catherine's Hill, they noticed a young woman standing at the top. Abby's father stopped and offered the woman a ride. Although Abby was huddled in her blanket, she heard the door on her side open and close, and she had to sit up so her father could push her seat forward to allow the hitchhiker into the back. Abby's father, however, drove only a few feet when he realized the young woman wasn't in the car, but was still standing in the road. He turned around, drove back to the woman and apologized, and for a second time let her into the car. Abby recounts the following: "I know she got in that time because I saw her feet when I looked between the seats. I remember because she was wearing what they used to call high tops, boots that laced up. As we drove off down the road, Daddy was talking away to the woman in the back, but I was not paying any attention. Suddenly, he stopped the car, got out, and flipped the seat back forward. As I looked at the back seat, Daddy was wiping water off the vinyl seat. No one was there."

A particularly chilling close encounter with Catherine happened to Dale Whitney, a musician who had finished playing in Bar Harbor one evening and was traveling alone to Machias. As Dale describes it, he was just cresting Catherine's Hill when he saw a young woman standing on the peak of the road ahead of him, the very spot on the road before it takes the deep plunge down the mountain. The girl he saw was dressed in a diaphanous gown. And no, she wasn't headless. In fact, at first Dale had no idea he was looking at a phantom. When he stopped the car and rolled down a window to see what she wanted, the young woman leaned in, smiled softly, and said, "I need a man to take me to Bar Harbor." Dale had just come from Bar Harbor—an hour's drive—and he was tired, having played all night. As he describes it, he was weighing in his mind what to do next when he noticed that he could see through the woman. Ever so faintly, he could see the white line painted on the road directly behind her. In horror, he looked at the pretty face only a few feet away from him, still leaning in his window and waiting for a reply to her breathless request. Completely shaken, he managed to blurt out, "I just came from there," before accelerating his car and speeding away.

By the time Dale reached the bottom of the mountain, only moments later, he reconsidered his actions and doubted his senses. "I figured I must have been tired and that my eyes were playing tricks on me. And I began to worry about the girl I had just left in the road." So Dale turned around, but when he arrived at the top of Catherine's Hill again, the young woman had vanished. Stopping his car, Dale called out, but received no reply. It dawned on him that he had just brushed up against the famous ghost of Black's Woods. Amazed and wide awake, Dale drove straight to Machias. But the story doesn't end there. On the same day, Dale had business that required him to drive back through Black's Woods towards Ellsworth. It was a beautiful day now, and the ghostly events from hours before seemed impossibly remote. But when Dale reached the top of Catherine's Hill, he found he was dead wrong. Exactly in the spot where he had seen Catherine standing, Dale was shocked to see a terrible accident—a van overturned and totaled. "No one in that vehicle could have survived," he later stated. "At least I can't imagine how." Could this accident be attributed to the ghost of Catherine? We will never know, but one thing is certain: be prepared to see her yourself if you take The Black's Woods Road, especially on a misty, moonlit night. And if indeed you do see Catherine, remember not to follow your instinct to flee in terror. Your safety lies in offering a ride to the horrifying apparition.

2

Bloodstains

S ome ghost stories are more frightening than others, and the following tale from Jonesboro, Maine, is among the worst. A ghastly murder, bloodstains that cannot be removed, and a vengeful spirit that comes in with the fog make this story unforgettable. The setting is a beautiful coastal house, by all appearances a dream home, but in reality something out of a nightmare. Here a horrifying past comes alive, and a future even more terrifying unfolds before our eyes.

What is it about fog that makes it reoccur as a motif in so many ghost stories? Perhaps fog merely exaggerates the sense of the unknown, truly the deepest source of human fear. In the same way that shadows are frightening, fog keeps us literally "in the dark," blinding us to a danger that may be no more than a few feet away. While this is true, there might be something more to fog than the mystery it instills. Some theories of the paranormal posit the necessity of fog, or some kind of vapor, in most supernatural manifestations. Through the medium of fog, disembodied spirits are given a kind of temporary substance. We may never know the truth of such claims, but as Crystal Czaja put it, "when heavy fog rolls in, things begin to get strange."

Crystal never lived in the house in Jonesboro, but she knew the young couple who did, a couple we'll call John and Elaine. Crystal writes that, "when they moved in, a murder had just been committed. It had occurred so recently that they had to take the police tape down when they moved in. Apparently, what they were told was that a woman went crazy and murdered her husband in the downstairs bedroom. The couple wasn't told any of the details, just that it happened. Last we all knew, the woman was still on trial for it."

In that small downstairs bedroom, located just off the kitchen, the floor was still stained with blood from the recent murder. The owner of the house informed John and Elaine that because of its history, he was willing to rent the gorgeous home for next to nothing. He asked, however, that they replace the floor in the downstairs bedroom, an easy task since the room was small. John and Elaine were initially apprehensive about renting a home that had been the scene of a grisly murder, but the killer was now in custody; besides, the young couple had no need to use the little bedroom, which they could shut off and keep for storage. So after a short reflection, John and Elaine accepted the offer to rent the house. The owner, delighted to have the place occupied, which might lessen its awful stigma, quickly went his own way.

Until the fog rolled in, nothing unusual occurred. Then one evening when Elaine was alone for a few hours, the fog came in off the sea, blanketing the house and everything around it. While she was in the kitchen, Elaine thought she heard something from the small bedroom nearby. It sounded like a dull scuffle, like someone was in there. Quietly, she went to the door of the bedroom, and, by listening carefully, she heard faint, stealth-like scuffling sounds within. Her heart beating, she opened the door to the room where the murder had taken place. The bedroom was empty, but Elaine distinctly felt something brush past her when she opened the door.

When John returned that evening, Elaine described to him what happened, so the next morning he went to check out the downstairs bedroom. He was totally unprepared for what he saw. There on the newly replaced floor were exact replicas of the bloodstains left from the murder. Deeply disturbed, John tried to clean the stains, but they could not be removed. There was only one thing to do: replace the flooring again. The room's size made the job easy; in any case, he and Elaine couldn't bear to see the stains there, especially now that they had reappeared so inexplicably.

Approximately a month later, Elaine was alone in the house again when heavy fog returned. This time, Elaine was in the living room when she was unexpectedly alarmed. Through the room's glass patio doors, she thought she saw a dark figure lurking in the fog outside. The image appeared like a flash, and then it was gone. The only way to the deck was through the house, so Elaine was understandably confused as well as upset. Then she heard something coming from the downstairs bedroom near the kitchen. The sounds were the same as the last time—the noise of a dull, muted scuffle. When Elaine opened the door to look inside the room, she once again felt something distinctly brush past her. Shaken, she checked the house to make sure all the doors and windows were locked. Only then did she go upstairs to bed to wait for John, falling asleep before he came home.

The next morning John scolded Elaine for having left the whole house unlocked. When he returned the night before, he had found all the doors open. This was impossible to explain since Elaine had carefully closed down the house, locking each door and checking it before heading to bed. Then, a few days later, the bloodstains reappeared—they had bled through the new floor. Once again, exact replicas of the original stains marked the floor of the downstairs bedroom. Completely exasperated, John didn't replace the flooring this time. He simply covered the stains with a throw rug.

About a month later, events took a terrifying turn. Fog again shrouded the home in Jonesboro. As in the previous cases, Elaine was alone in the house for a few hours. Naturally, she felt uneasy, but the evening started off with no unusual incidents. Then, when she was in the kitchen, she heard those strange, muffled sounds of a struggle coming from the small bedroom. As if she were in a nightmare doomed to repeat itself, Elaine approached the door of the room and opened it, cringing as she felt that same malevolent force rush past her. Walking into the bedroom to look around, Elaine tripped on the throw rug that covered the persistent bloodstains. She fell to the floor, hitting her head hard enough to knock her unconscious. John returned soon afterwards and, to his horror, found Elaine sprawled on the floor of the downstairs bedroom, the horrible dark stains spread out below her. He quickly revived her and prepared to take her to the hospital. Then the couple noticed other truly mystifying details.

To begin with, the throw rug had disappeared. Unaccountably, it was not in the room, nor was it anywhere in the house. To this day, John and Elaine can't explain how it could have disappeared. Even more disturbing, Elaine suffered injuries beyond those to her head. All over her body were small wounds and cuts that could not be explained by falling as she did. The doctors in Machias were at a loss to account for the lacerations. It looked as if Elaine had been assaulted, but she had been alone in the house, and an intruder could be ruled out since the home was entirely locked up when John returned that evening. Too frightened to spend another night in the house in Jonesboro, John and Elaine packed their belongings and fled from the place before anything else could occur.

It is fortunate they left when they did, because all events pointed to supernatural reenactments of the original murder. What else could explain the persistent bloodstains, the muted sounds of a scuffle, and the strange wounds all over Elaine's body? Strangely, though, it was now a woman—Elaine herself—who was the victim. Could it be that the spirit of the murdered man was returning to the house to seek revenge, either mistaking Elaine for the woman who killed him, or simply targeting her as a substitute? If so, it was probably his vengeful spirit that was seen as the dark figure lurking on the deck, and it was probably the spirit of the same man experienced as a sensation of something brushing past Elaine when she opened the door of the downstairs bedroom. John and Elaine never learned if the strange events continued when new tenants moved into the house. As far we know, the bloodstains still mark the floor of the downstairs bedroom, and events take a horrifying turn every time the fog rolls in from the sea.

3
The Floating Doll

There is a quality about dolls that some people find creepy. Perhaps it is their painted smiles and their wide-eyed, frozen expressions. Or, possibly, it is because, at the most primitive level of our beings, there is a lurking suspicion that dolls are not really inanimate at all. At one time in human history, dolls were not mere toys, but objects imbued with religious and mystical significance. This tradition survives today mainly in the form of the voodoo doll. The doll in this story, however, was just an ordinary, modern doll and was hardly frightening in a supernatural sense—until it began moving by itself.

A haunted sea-captain's house in Eastport, Maine, is the setting for this strange tale. Built on Water Street to overlook the ships in the once-bustling harbor, the house had been abandoned for many years until it was purchased by the parents of Lacey Bunnell. Shortly after being inhabited again, the house gave irrefutable signs of restless spirits. Lacey recounts that at night it was common to hear footsteps downstairs moving from room to room long after everyone had gone to bed. Often, objects would inexplicably be moved. Once, when Lacey's mother and father were wallpapering upstairs, a bizarre incident occurred. The elderly couple had just pasted on a row or two of the wallpaper when they were interrupted and had to leave the room. When they returned, they were shocked to see that the newly applied wallpaper was covered with scratches; it had been torn up moments after being applied. There was no one else in the house, and the couple did not own any pets. Apparently, the spirits in the house didn't approve of the wallpaper.

Incidents like these encouraged Lacey and her mother to research the history of the house, which was built in 1864. They discovered that one of the original owners had a daughter who, with her governess, died in a carriage accident. It began to seem like the little girl was still occupying the old house on Water Street.

Events culminated in the summer of 1989, when Lacey often visited the house with her two children: Samantha, who was four years old, and her brother Joshua, who was seven. Whenever Samantha would visit her grandmother's house, the little girl would play with an imaginary friend. Samantha called this companion Elizabeth. It was not uncommon for Elizabeth to accompany Samantha the whole time she was visiting her grandparents.

Lacey and her mother came to believe that Elizabeth was not imaginary at all, but actually the spirit of the little girl who had once lived in the house. To avoid frightening her daughter, Lacey did not mention this to Samantha. It is significant, however, that Elizabeth never followed Samantha back to her own house. The imaginary friend appeared only in the old sea-captain's dwelling. In this house there was an upstairs bedroom that had the look and atmoshere of a nursery, and when Lacey's mother bought the house, she made it into a bedroom and playroom for her two grandchildren. In all likelihood, this was the same room once occupied by the girl whose spirit was known as Elizabeth.

In August the strangest event of all occurred. Lacey had brought Samantha and Joshua over to visit their grandmother for the day. Most of the morning Samantha played upstairs, and occasionally Lacey could hear her chattering away. Whether the little girl was talking to Elizabeth or lending her voice to the dolls she was playing with, Lacey didn't know, but at first nothing seemed unusual. When it came time for lunch, Lacey sent Joshua upstairs to get his sister. He wasn't gone long before he returned with a strange look on his face. He told his mother, "You better come back upstairs. You're going to want to come and see this." His attitude and tone of voice indicated that something out of the ordinary was taking place.

Lacey, followed by her mother and Joshua, quietly climbed the front staircase. Samantha was engaged in play and didn't notice her mother, grandmother, and brother standing in the hallway directly outside the children's room. The door to the room was open, and when they looked inside, Lacey and her mother had the shock of a lifetime. As Lacey put it, "There was Samantha sitting on the floor, playing with her dolls. This in itself was not unique or strange; she often played alone with her dolls. The odd thing is that she was not alone. Samantha was holding up one doll, moving it and talking, while there was another one moving in a similar way all by itself."

The floating doll was suspended in the air at a height level with Samantha's face and was approximately eight inches away from the child. The doll didn't just hover there, however. Its arms and legs were moving as if it were being animated by an invisible being. Three people witnessed the event—Joshua, his mother, and his grandmother. As for little Samantha, she didn't see the doll as suspended in the air; Samantha was seeing someone holding it up there, someone no one else could see.

As calmly as possible, Lacey asked Samantha what she was doing. The instant that Lacey spoke, the floating doll dropped to the floor.

In response to her mother's inquiry, Samantha answered that she was "just playing with Elizabeth."

Later, Lacey questioned Samantha more closely about her "imaginary" friend Elizabeth. From the little-girl's description, we can picture Elizabeth as approximately eight years old. She had "pin-curled hair," in Samantha's words, and a "frilly white dress with blue ribbons." By all accounts, she must have looked like the girl who had died in the carriage accident more than a hundred years before. For a while after this incident, Samantha continued to play with Elizabeth, but there were no other events as strange and disturbing as the floating doll.

Reflection on the event makes it clear that the house on Water Street was subject to poltergeist activity. This can be seen in the objects that were mysteriously moved, the strange scratches on the wallpaper, and especially in the doll that was suspended in the old nursery on that August afternoon. Apparently, Elizabeth was a lonely spirit seeking no more than the companionship of another child. As Samantha grew older, Elizabeth made fewer and fewer appearances, until it seemed that she had moved on, finally leaving the house she once inhabited, perhaps because she had no children to play with. Nonetheless, the story of the floating doll urges us to reconsider what is often characterized as child's play. How many other spirits are dismissed as mere figments of a child's imagination? Perhaps from the perspective of the spirit known as Elizabeth, the living child Samantha was the imaginary friend. For all we know, the living appear like spirits to the dead. This we may never know, but one thing is certain—even an ordinary doll can be absolutely terrifying if animated by the dead.

4

The Children Of The Fill

A horrifying secret discovered beneath a newly built home culminates in this ghost story from Steuben, on the coast of Maine. This ghastly account involves the ordeal of the dead visiting and threatening the living, objects moving on their own accord and witnessed by several individuals, and a strange, cryptic warning from a Ouija board that confirmed the nightmares of a child. Tammy Cox and Julia Dodwell collected this terrifying tale for me from a woman we'll refer to as Alice. It concerns her sister Meredith and her family.

During the 1990s, Meredith and her husband built a home in Steuben for themselves and their three daughters. The house is a large, shingled contemporary with a wraparound deck offering beautiful views of Eagle Hill. Located at the head of Gouldsboro Bay, Steuben is a small fishing and summer residential community. Named for a leader in the Revolutionary War, the town was incorporated in the late eighteenth century. Like many rural Maine communities, Steuben contains old family burial plots scattered in meadows or swallowed up by encroaching forests, but none of these cemeteries were located on the three-acre lot where the house was built—or so Meredith and her husband thought.

Shortly after moving into their new home, Meredith and her family began to experience strange events, such as the mysterious displacement of common household items. Once, for example, when she was alone in the house, Meredith was using a calculator at her desk. Suddenly, inexplicably, the calculator was gone. She searched the desk thoroughly, then the room as well, but the calculator was nowhere to be found. Finally, she left the room for a few minutes, and when she returned, the calculator was sitting in the middle of her desk.

During the family's first four years in their house, this kind of poltergeist activity became commonplace. Then, for reasons that are still unknown, it accelerated dramatically.

One morning in winter, when no one was at the house, a friend came over to drop off some wreathing brush. As Meredith's sister writes, "He opened the cellar door and went to deposit the brush. While he was down there, he could hear cupboards and doors slamming. He also heard the sounds of people walking across the floor." At first he thought some of the family members must be home, but when he called out, no one answered him. Thinking this odd, he telephoned Meredith later on and asked her why no one came down when he was at the house. Meredith was surprised because she and the rest of her family were not home that day. Worried that there might have been an intruder, she searched the first and second floors of the house, which had been locked, and nothing seemed out of place; certainly nothing had been stolen. Disturbed by the sounds her friend had heard, Meredith decided to set up a video camera while she was out. While the camera never captured any images, it did record more sounds of cupboards and doors opening and slamming.

Around this time, Meredith's youngest daughter, Amanda, began acting uncharacteristically. The five year old developed a sudden aversion to her bedroom. She started wetting her bed, something she had never done before, and she began having a hard time going to sleep in her own room. Night after night, the girl would leave her room and climb into her parents' bed.

When they asked their daughter what was wrong, she insisted that she no longer liked her room and didn't want to stay there anymore. Eventually, however, she admitted that she was having awful dreams in her room, but she could not recall for her parents the details of these nightmares. Children often go through experiences that parents may never understand or know about, so at first Meredith and her husband thought Amanda was going through an emotional phase that would soon pass. Unbeknownst to them at the time, this behavior would last for nearly six months.

Then one night the girl finally revealed the true nature of her nightmares. Amanda declared, "They're jumping on my bed—they're jumping on my bed!"

"Who is?" her mother asked in alarm.

"The little kids," the daughter answered.

Amanda went on to add more gruesome details. She complained that there were children who visited her at night. They climbed on her bed and crowded around her. She described feeling suffocated by the children. As the little girl put it, her nightmare visitors had taken her socks and were stuffing them down her throat. In fear, the girl fled her room for the solace and safety of her parents.

At a loss to explain what was happening in her new house, Meredith consulted a Ouija board. The oracle spelled out a strange warning that confirmed the dreams Amanda was having. It claimed that there were four other children in the house besides Amanda and her sisters. These children were in Amanda's room. The Ouija board then warned Meredith that something would happen to her youngest daughter. As Amanda's aunt Alice writes, "Thankfully, nothing did." Nonetheless, for safe measure, Meredith moved Amanda into a new bedroom.

Now if the house in Steuben were old, like most of the homes in the village, Meredith might have concluded that the spirits of former residents were haunting the place. This, however, could not be the case; Meredith and her husband had broken new ground to have their house built. The next step was to make some discrett inquiries about the contractor they had hired to build the house. That is when they discovered that the Town of Steuben was investigating this individual for disturbing a cemetery. Alice writes, "As it turns out, the dirt used to fill in where the house was to be put during the building process was taken from a site that allegedly had been a burial ground of sorts, and the bones of these tormented souls were in the dirt under the house." The fill had probably come from an old family burial ground that was no longer in use. In all likelihood, the soil that was removed had contained the remains of children who had been buried many years ago.

Since Meredith and her husband made their gruesome discovery, the ghostly children have made few visits to the house in Steuben. Why they are staying away is anyone's guess—perhaps because the truth was finally discovered regarding the disturbance of their graves. Assuming it was the restless spirits of these children who were opening and slamming doors, we might conclude that they were doing more than simply making their presence known. The message being communicated seems to be the experience of claustrophobia, the sensation of being trapped and the desire for escape. This theory is supported by the most unsettling detail of this entire affair—Amanda's experience of being suffocated. Were the phantoms of children forcing her to undergo the sensation of being in the grave? If so, the horror of this tale deepens. For spirits tied to their bodies' remains, interment is no different than being buried alive.

5

Mills Cove and Other Haunted Beaches

Down East Maine contains miles of untouched beaches. When seen on a shining summer day, these beaches are striking for their sheer scenic beauty. Wooded shorelines captivate the senses with the roar of crashing surf, the endless views, and a constant sea breeze that smells of salt and beach roses. Charmed by the cries of the gulls, we may neglect the sad lament of the mourning dove or the foreboding call of the owl, which hoots a warning according to local folklore. But when seen by the light of the moon, a beach has a far-different character than it does during the day. The same can be said for a beach seen in the middle of winter, when the deep freeze makes "sea smoke" rise like phantoms from the water. Yes, the beaches here have many sides to them. Some of these sides are sinister, horrifying, and definitely dangerous. The lonely stretches of ledge and sand contain more than their share of ghostly encounters and ghastly outcomes.

Haunted beaches are particularly plentiful on islands. Maybe this is because of the old notion that ghosts can't cross water. Or, perhaps, it is because islands were the perfect places to bury treasure or dispose of a body.

The infamous Sable Island, near the Bay of Fundy, has a beach no one would want to visit at midnight under a full moon. The island is home to more than three hundred fifty shipwrecks, reminders that beaches are the places where wrecks and their tragic human cargo have washed up over the years, giving rise to many legends involving ghosts or lost souls stalking the shores.

Accidents are bad enough, but murder or foul play is far worse. Consider, for example, the beach at Mills Cove, which is located on Campobello Island, only a short bridge away from Lubec, Maine. This story was told to me by Helen Smith, who heard the tale from her mother-in-law. A more ghastly ghost story would be hard to come by. The Mills Cove legend concerns a man who killed his wife, chopped her into pieces, and packed her remains in an old barrel, like those used to hold herring. Then, the murderous husband took the barrel out to sea and dropped it overboard. Apparently, however, the sea drove the barrel back onto the shore in Mills Cove, where it broke open; thus, the murder was discovered. According to local legend, on foggy nights or when the moon is full, the spirit of the murdered woman wanders hopelessly along the shore.

Buried treasure has given rise to many a tale involving ghosts on island beaches. On Cross Island, located off the coast of Jonesboro, there are seven graves, and according to Fred Watts anyone visiting them is likely to be scared off by the sound of clanking chains. Watts describes a legendary treasure chest buried somewhere in a cave accessible only from the beach at low tide. Treasure hunters should beware, for the treasure may be guarded or come at too high a cost. According to Watts, "Some believe there is some connection between the graves and the treasure chest."

Then there is the coastline of Big Libby Island, also home to ghost stories involving buried treasure and foul play, this time in the form of a wicked man named Pettegrew. He and his sons built a road from Big Libby Island to Little Libby Island. Fred Watts states that, "He worked his boys so hard that two of them became crippled and both were drowned." Rumor had it that Pettegrew had amassed a large fortune through sheer villainy. At night he "tolled vessels onto the rocks with a signal light. He would salvage the cargo after killing the crew." Because he built a road to Little Libby Island, some locals believe he buried his ill-gotten gains there. One can only imagine the tormented souls doomed to walk these shores for eternity—the wretched family, the ghastly patriarch, and his long trail of mournful victims.

Moving onto the mainland, we head to one of the few sand beaches in the area. It's located in Roque Bluffs, only a few miles from Machias. The beautiful seaside setting is home to a state park. In the summer the *Rosa rugosa* are in full bloom, the sea grass blows freely in the wind, and the curving sandy beach is rarely overcrowded. It would be hard to find a more picturesque place, yet Roque Bluffs, too, has its legends of restless spirits. The beach is home to a ghostly companion known only as a set of footprints and the sound of someone approaching. The question remains, is this ghost a good-natured companion or a stalker from another world?

One August day, Audrey Dufour and her mother went to the beach at Roque Bluffs to collect rocks and shells for crafts. Audrey states that "It was a windy and slightly cold day, and when my mother and I arrived at the beach, we found that we were the only ones there." The sand was smooth from the receding tide and lack of visitors that day. Audrey and her mother walked along, talking and collecting treasures from the sea. When her mother moved ahead to look at something she had spotted, Audrey had a strange encounter. She writes, "I heard what sounded like someone walking up behind me." When she looked over her shoulder, no one was there. Then, as she headed toward her mother, she heard someone walking behind her again. She writes, "This time I turned completely around. I didn't see anyone, but when I looked down, I saw my mother's set of footprints, my set of footprints, along with a third set following me." But the story gets stranger, for the third set of footprints continued to appear on the beach. As Audrey walked to her mother, she looked back in horror to see a third set of footprints forming themselves in the sand. The incident ended abruptly after Audrey called out to her mother.

Jasper Beach is located outside Bucks Harbor. This secluded town beach is one of the most unique and untouched shorefronts in the region. The entire beach is made up of smooth jasper stones. Even on the hottest days of summer, the air blows cool and threatens to unleash the damp fog from the sea. While the rugged beauty of Jasper Beach is striking, the shore has seen its share of tragedies and has been the setting for several suicides. One young woman, for example, was persuaded to turn State's evidence against individuals who had preyed upon her innocence. After agreeing, she discovered she would have to confront these same individuals in court. This was apparently too much for the high-strung girl, who took her own life one night on Jasper Beach. Is it the girl or some other hapless suicide who haunts the shore with a wailing cry often mistaken for the sound of the wind. But old-timers will tell you of another apparition here, the vengeful spirit of a murderous man.

Local legend has it that no one can stay the night safely at Jasper Beach. The threat comes in the form of a wrathful ghost. Apparently, a ladies' man used the beach for romantic liaisons. One night he went to a bar in the Machias area, picked up a beautiful woman named Dina, and spent the night with her on Jasper Beach. What he didn't know was that Dina had just broken up with a violent and jealous man. When Dina's ex-boyfriend discovered where she had been, he took her lover back to Jasper Beach, tied him up, and executed him. The killer escaped detection, and the ghost of his victim still roams the beach. According to legend, this spirit will try to inflict its fate on anyone foolhardy enough to spend the night on this bleak shore.

The legendary Phantom of the Narrows takes us to Look's Point in Jonesboro. There on the rocky and grassy shore appears a ghost that is a forerunner of impending war. It is the apparition of Nell Kilton, who as a young woman had fallen in love with a Native American man. Upon the discovery of his daughter's love, Nell's father murdered the man and banished his daughter, who went to live with the Passamaquoddy people in the area. She never married and became a prophet or seer, predicting the French and Indian War and the American Revolution. Her involvement in the fight for independence led to her capture and execution by the British for being a revolutionary spy. On the scaffold, Nell allegedly vowed to revisit the American people whenever war was imminent. Apparently, she kept her promise. On Kilton Neck, in the narrows that lead out to Englishman Bay, the specter has appeared to foretell the War of 1812, the Mexican War, the Civil War, and World Wars I and II. Facing the water, her long hair blowing back from her face, Nell's phantom waves her arms and shouts the Passamaquoddy war whoop, which echoes ominously down the shore.

In many ways, ancient Native Americans still people the coastline of Down East Maine. Their presence is denoted by a stone spearhead washed up by the surf, a clam midden buried under the blackberries and purple vetch, or a rock-mounded grave belonging to the Red Paint People, ancestors of the present-day tribes in the region. Along the rocky shores of Machiasport are enigmatic petroglyphs, or pictures carved into the stone. Some of these images are more than three thousand years old and speak of a time when the spirit world was always close at hand; a time of shamans, ancestral spirits, and the totems of clans. One petroglyph on the east side of Machias Bay depicts a phantom-like winged figure. Beneath it are the shapes of four humans holding hands. Could this be the depiction of an ancient supernatural sighting on these shores?

No matter how we view them or in what context we think of them, the beaches of Down East Maine are haunting for more than their rugged beauty and rich history. Wraiths wander the strand, from different times and cultures, and in this sense, the coastline is as much theirs as ours.

6

The Murdering Ghost of Dennysville

Of all the tales of the supernatural, few are more horrifying than the legend of the murdering ghost of Dennysville, a spirit that clearly defies the adage that the dead can't hurt you; only the living can. This malevolent ghost occupied an old Dennysville house and appears to have premeditated—and accomplished—an actual death. Worse yet, the victim was a child.

The story starts in March 1976 when Eileen Campbell, a young mother in her twenties, received a call from her husband, who was in Maine searching for a new home for his family. He called to say he had found the perfect place in the town of Dennysville. Filled with excitement, Eileen packed her two toddlers into her 1968 Chevy and headed Down East. She and her husband had wanted to get out of the city to raise their children in a safe environment. As Eileen writes, "Boston was becoming unlivable, unemployment was rampant, and school bussing had turned the city into a racial war zone. A post-war, back-to-the-land movement was on, and we wanted out."

The house seemed perfect, or most of it did, to be accurate. The two-hundred-year-old Cape sat on five acres on the outskirts of the village, a short walk from a bend in the Dennys River. The house had originally been a tavern and had been located one half mile away, on the top of a knoll overlooking the river. It had been moved when a church was built on the original site. Eileen writes, "I liked the look and feel of the low, barn-red house surrounded by bushes of red and white roses, a strawberry patch in the dooryard, and rows of cultivated raspberries." There was only one problem—a tiny back bedroom upstairs with one window overlooking the driveway on the north side of the house.

Eileen writes that "When the door was opened to the little room, I was totally unprepared for the blast of cold that met us. It was not a damp, unlived-in cold like the rest of the house, but an airless, vault-like cold that froze me at the doorway. I peeked in, took notice of the dingy window and what looked like an old chimney tucked in one corner. I didn't like the room at all." The rest of the house had a sunny, inviting atmosphere, so Eileen tried to dismiss her aversion to the back bedroom. She and her husband bought the house in Dennysville for next to nothing and moved in. By August a new addition to her family had arrived—a beautiful baby named Jaclyn.

As long as possible, Eileen put off settling the children into their new room upstairs. It was the tiny back bedroom that caused her trepidation. Although she had no intention of moving her children into that particular room, it was simply too close for comfort: only an old door with a rusty hook-style latch separated it from the room destined to be her children's. As winter approached, Eileen's husband began to pressure her to shift the children into their room upstairs. "When I mentioned to him that the northern corner room smelled funny and felt strange, made me uneasy in a way I couldn't explain, he told me I had been watching too much TV, that my head was going soft, that my imagination had run away with me. I tended to believe him about everything." Eileen blocked off the connecting door to the small, cold bedroom with a diaper-changing table and finally moved her children upstairs. Strange events began to occur soon afterward.

They started when Eileen began noticing that the latch on the door to the back bedroom was inexplicably off its hook in the mornings. The latch was too high for any of her children to unhook, and her husband swore he hadn't touched it. Yet on more mornings than not, the door would be unhooked. Then she began finding the door to the back room open. At first it was ajar only an inch or two. Then, on later occasions, the door was open three or four inches, then half a foot, and so on, until it was nearly wide open. When Eileen mentioned to her husband that the door was unhooking itself and opening, he dismissed it as the actions of an old house adjusting to the cold, like old foundations heaved up by frost. Eileen writes, "I bought this explanation because I wanted to, because it sounded good, not because I believed it was the real answer." Slowly at first, an unspoken terror was taking hold of the young mother.

Then her nightmares commenced, and they were always the same. In them, Eileen held one of her children lying limp in her arms. When she looked down, she could see that the child was dead. "Their faces and the external situation changed each time, but my reaction was the same," Eileen writes. "I would wake sharply from the bad end of the dream, often on the inhale of a sob." Now everyone who knows Eileen will tell you she is an eternal optimist—never in her life had she experienced dreams like these. It got so that she was afraid to fall asleep; inevitably she would find herself back in the same dream, holding a dead child. Night after night, the horrible dreams took place while the back bedroom door unhooked itself and creaked open.

In January and February the dreams became more insistent, until Eileen had the strangest, most horrifying nightmare of all. It began like all the others. She was standing and holding a child, one she knew was dead. When she finally looked down, she could not identify the child in her arms. The face, as she recalls, was smudged, or blurred, like someone had partially rubbed it out with an eraser. Then, in her dream, she heard a voice, a deep, booming voice. It uttered one word that still echoes in her mind.

"Choose!"

In terror, the young mother woke up whispering, "I can't." She writes, "It was all I could reply. One of my kids was at stake. I considered that maybe I was just going crazy. That would be easier to bear than to ever have to make such a choice as the growling voice demanded." This time her fear was such that she knew she had to do something. The next morning, she moved the changing table and marched into the airless bedroom.

Eileen remembers closing her eyes and speaking in her mind to whatever was dark and threatening and abhorrent in the place. "Get out. Please go. Go now. In the name of God, go away now!" When Eileen opened her eyes, she didn't expect to see anything. Then, in a corner of the room under the sloping eaves, she saw the flash of a dark, withered figure that "exuded a heart-numbing sorrow crumpled into a pitiful ball on a small chair in the corner near the chimney," Eileen writes. "I couldn't tell you if it was male or female. The image was gone in a shifting heartbeat, leaving only the dusty corner. There was no chair there at all. I knew then that I had seen something." After that, the dreams abruptly ceased. While Eileen believed that this change was due to the confrontation she had in the back bedroom, the events that followed indicate a far more sinister reason. With the nightmares unexpectedly gone, Eileen was lulled into a false sense of security.

From there the story wraps up quickly, as tragedies often do. In early spring, a month after the nightmares ended, Eileen's baby, Jaclyn, developed meningitis, but the young doctor at the little regional hospital in Machias misdiagnosed the illness. He informed Eileen that the infant's fever was due to teething and the flu, and he urged her to keep down the fever. Only hours later, Jaclyn's fever spiked uncontrollably, and she began convulsing. Eileen rushed her to the hospital. The baby was airlifted to Portland to a pediatric intensive-care unit, but help came too late. By the end of the day, Eileen was holding her dead baby in her arms. Her nightmares had come true.

Beside herself with grief, Eileen returned to Dennysville. She walked into that house and marched up the stairs and into the back bedroom, and that is when she received her final surprise—the dark, ominous feeling was gone, and the room felt just as warm and cheerful as the rest of the house. Eileen writes, "there was nothing there. No vault-like air, no cloying, emotional presence. Nothing." Something in the room had demanded the life of one of her children. With that accomplished, the presence departed, never to return. The final twist was the bright, sunny atmosphere in the room. It indicated that a dark and diabolical transaction had indeed taken place.

7

The Return of the Kettle Tinker

One recurring character in the ghost stories of Down East Maine is the murdered peddler or tinker. Perhaps these colorful individuals turn up so frequently because they were once a regular part of the New England landscape, traveling from house to house to sell their wares or mend broken pots and pans. Or it may be that peddlers and tinkers were the quintessential outsiders, links to a larger world, "people from away" who, by definition, brought into stark relief the isolation of small Maine communities. Or maybe it was simply the awful drama of their vulnerability and susceptibility to harm. Indeed, the traveling peddler was alone in the world, often without nearby kin, a prey to both murderous individuals and the savagery of nature; far too often caught without warning by an unexpected storm, a quickly descending nightfall, or a treacherous hand. Now more prevalent as ghosts than as real individuals, peddlers or tinkers deserve our pity and our fear.

In the town of Cooper, a ghastly legend exists involving the murder of a peddler who sold watches and jewelry and whose spirit fought for more than a century to escape the house in which he was killed. The tale begins when the peddler, caught in the falling darkness, sought shelter at a house owned by the Gooch family. A couple of weeks later, his body was discovered, stuffed down an old well close to the Gooch homestead. The man's throat was cut, and his possessions were gone. Years later, when Mrs. Gooch grew elderly and perhaps senile, she would make ominous statements such as "What would you think if you saw two men go down to the basement and only one come up?"

The Gooch home was later purchased by Rowena Bates and her husband, and apparently there was one door in the house that could not be kept closed. Even when the door was tied shut, it was always found open the next day. Could it be that the unfortunate peddler was trying to leave? Eventually, the house was torn down, and a new one built, finally releasing the restless spirit.

Topsfield is the setting of another peddler's spirit. One evening, a weary peddler stopped at a local inn and requested shelter for the night. The place was full, but the innkeepers offered him a room in the attic, which he gratefully accepted. According to Octavia Dowling, "In the night something happened to the peddler. He was found dead the next morning. The town officials took away his body, but his spirit remained behind. Each time a lamp was taken into the attic room, it was blown out." Rumors spread throughout the small community, and soon the inn began losing business. When electricity came to Topsfield, the owners of the inn thought they had a solution to their problem. They wired the house and the attic. But, as Octavia writes, "The lights worked beautifully—all but the one in *his* room. It just won't stay on!"

The most unique of tinker spirits, however, resides in Columbia Falls. He is known as the kettle tinker, and his unfortunate spirit can actually be summoned by people passing the house in which he died. Columbia Falls is a picturesque hamlet that looks as if time stopped there more than a century ago. It contains a cluster of big, old shingled homes around a town square featuring an imposing edifice known as the Ruggles House. The building, which is open to the public in the summer months, has its own ghost stories. According to Samantha Berst, who worked there as a guide, after visiting hours one can sometimes hear the voices of children in the house, which at one time served as a school. The setting of our tale is a more modest dwelling located a few miles away.

On the Centerville Road in Columbia Falls stands a big, yellow two-story house with a huge barn and a shed attached. The home sits on a hill located close to the old Pineo Mill. This is the setting for one of the most grisly of murders, and one of the most dramatic of hauntings.

The story starts in the fall of 1801, on a brilliant October afternoon when a tinker who was selling and fixing kettles stopped at the two-story dwelling and asked the mistress of the house if he could have some dinner and stay the night. The woman served the tinker a hearty meal, which, unfortunately, was his last. When the farmer who owned the house returned, events took a nasty turn. Perhaps, the farmer suspected that the tinker had committed adultery, or perhaps he thought the tinker had stolen something. At any rate, a terrible fight broke out and the kettle tinker was murdered.

Not content with killing the man, the farmer dismembered the corpse, cutting off the head and chopping the body into small pieces. The bloody remains were placed in an empty whiskey barrel, which the farmer then rolled down a set of steps from the barn into the shed. Even in 1801, the shed was run down, with only a dirt floor. Here the farmer started digging, burying the barrel with the remains of the kettle tinker. No doubt the murderer hoped to cover up forever his bloody deed. The irony would be that the spirit could never be quelled, contained, or even forgotten, because he could be summoned.

Since then, old timers have claimed that anyone can conjure the spirit of the kettle tinker. Apparently, if you stop in front of the house where he was killed and dare the spirit to appear, he will pass by the window. Be patient, however. It may be that you have to call to the spirit more than once, but persistence will pay off, and eventually you will see him.

Growing up in the area and knowing the story of the kettle tinker, Jody Marston and some of her friends decided to test the truth of the matter for themselves. They drove to the house one autumn day when leaves were falling all around the abandoned building. Jody writes that "We parked the car beside the road and rolled down the window. I know we called to the tinker at least twenty times before we finally double-dog-dared him to come by the window.

"All of a sudden we heard the sound of a barrel rolling down the stairs. We all looked up to see a foggy figure in the window. You could see the whole ghostly form of a man in the window, holding his head. Then it was gone, but the curtains were ruffling back and forth as if someone was moving them. Nobody had lived in the house for years, and the window was closed tight. We were so scared that we drove away going at least 75 miles an hour."

So when you're out and about in Down East Maine, sympathize with the tinker or peddler of yesteryear as he traveled with his load through the remote byways of the region inhabited by suspicious locals and cutthroats far from the long arm of the law. And if your travels happen to take you to Columbia Falls, think twice before you head down the old Centerville Road. If you stop in front of the big house on the hill and call out to the spirit who resides there, be careful what you wish for, because it may come true! Then, you can see for yourself the spirit of the kettle tinker appear to the thunder of a barrel rolling down stairs.

8

Phantoms of Eastport

Eastport, Maine, located on Moose Island, is home to some of the most chilling of ghost tales, which is not surprising since it is a place of extremes. As its name suggests, it is the easternmost city in the United States. It also contains the deepest harbor on the east coast. Visible from the city's waterfront is Old Sow, the largest whirlpool in the western hemisphere. History is alive in Eastport. The brick waterfront, for example, is virtually unchanged since 1887, when the city was rebuilt after its third devastating fire. But history is alive in a deeper, literal, and more horrifying sense—phantoms stalk the shores and the foggy streets of Eastport, apparitions of individuals from the town's history of tragedy, madness, and warfare.

Our first stop is the ruins of Fort Sullivan on Battery Hill, the setting for the tale of the legendary foghorn soldier. During the War of 1812, the British seized Eastport and held the city until 1818. An armada of war ships, including the *Ramillies*, the *Rover*, and the *Terror* overtook Fort Sullivan, which surrendered to the force. The British required all citizens of Eastport to swear an oath of allegiance to England, and the document containing this oath can still be seen at the Peavey Library. Eight hundred British soldiers were stationed in Eastport during the occupation.

On Battery Hill stand the remains of the powder house; nearby are the barracks, which have been converted into a museum. Frannie Mitchell Segien grew up in Eastport, close to the ruins of Fort Sullivan, and on many occasions she witnessed the phantom soldier. When the mist rolled in from the sea and the foghorn blew, the soldier was clearly visible. He appeared as the silhouette of a man standing at attention and holding a musket.

Many years later Frannie mentioned the incidents to her husband. She described the phantom and its frightening effect, so chilling that the hairs raised on the back of her neck. Her husband recalled seeing the same figure standing on Battery Hill. As a child, he considered that the silhouette belonged to the devil himself. Frannie and her husband agreed that they had witnessed the same phenomenon. If in doubt, we can see it for ourselves. Having spoken to Frannie about the story, Tanya Dickey writes, "Frannie told me that this sight could still be seen today by looking up to Battery Hill when the foghorn blows and the fog rolls in. There amidst the fog will be the British soldier."

Who was the foghorn soldier? During the British occupation, the common soldiers stationed in Eastport endured lives of abject misery. Punishment for transgressions was swift and exceedingly harsh. One soldier found drunk on duty received one hundred fifty lashes. Citizens of Eastport grew accustomed to hearing groans and screams coming from the jail—called the "black hole"—at Fort Sullivan. Not surprisingly, many soldiers ran away, and sometimes an entire guard deserted en masse.

While mortality was not high, there were untimely deaths. For example, four soldiers were found washed up on the shore of Moose Island after trying to defect. Two other soldiers perished in the flames of a guardhouse fire. Of all the deaths, however, one stands out as the source of the ghostly legend. The historian Lorenzo Sabine writes that only one British soldier committed a crime so terrible that he was sentenced to death. But before he could be executed, the soldier committed suicide. Owing to his solitary appearance and the feeling of dread that he imparts, the foghorn soldier is most likely the apparition of this condemned man.

Madness reigns in other histories of Eastport's supernatural world. During the nineteenth century, the mentally ill were often mistreated: It was customary for families to lock in their attics relatives who had gone insane. From this unfortunate practice, legends arose, some involving hapless souls who had been forgotten and left behind in buildings that were abandoned. To the already gothic look of Eastport's desolate streets with their empty homes were added generations of stories in which residents saw the spirits of the mad. As a case in point, in one incident that occurred during the 1940s, Frannie Mitchell Segion's father was walking past an old house already associated with the confinement of someone mentally ill. The house had been long abandoned and was falling into ruin. Feeling like someone was watching him, the man looked up and noticed a figure staring down at him from a third-story window. The person looked very "gray and sad." In a flash, the face was gone, but Frannie's father had no doubt that he had seen an apparition belonging to one of the forgotten.

Madness in Eastport also took the form of violence, which was not uncommon in the once-populous city. During the mid-1800s, Eastport was a major shipping center, second in importance only to the port of New York. Canneries and smokehouses employed many people in a way of life that has been lost. Over a century ago an abandoned smokehouse stood in the western part of the city and was the setting of a violent fight that broke out between two workers. In the end, one of the men was never seen again. Thereafter, according to residents of the city, the smokehouse was plagued by evil spirits, whose appearances were even reported in newspapers of the time. People witnessed strange lights and unearthly noises, but for many the most chilling development was a box of bones unearthed by clam diggers on the beach below the smokehouse. While some locals believed that the ghostly occurrences were caused by tramps living in the subterranean room below the smokehouse, other residents felt this circumstance couldn't explain all of the mysterious events that gave the smokehouse its dread reputation. Whatever the case, the smokehouse is no longer standing, and one can only wonder if the angry spirits associated with the place are still out there along the dark, wooded shores of Passamaquoddy Bay.

In a nineteenth-century sea-captain's mansion overlooking the waterfront in Eastport, the ghost of a forlorn child brings to life another somber episode of the community's history. During its days as a thriving port, the city saw an enormous volume of trade with parts of Europe, Africa, and Asia. With the wooden schooners that traveled to and from Eastport came deadly diseases that struck with no quarter both the poor and the affluent. Our last phantom of Eastport is a victim of this time period, the apparition of a young girl who died before her time.

During the twelve years that Janet Toth and her family lived in the Eastport mansion, they had many occasions to witness the lonely and vengeful specter. Whenever Janet or her family held a party, the ghost of the mansion would appear, usually on the night before the social event. Typically, the apparition would be wearing a party dress. Sometimes she would be seen peering down from the top of the stairs, and, once, she even curtsied before disappearing. From her appearance and behavior, Janet and her husband began to wonder if the apparition belonged to a little girl who had died before a party to be held in her honor, or if in life she simply thrived on the lavish galas and balls held in the stately home. Sometimes, however, the ghost was only visible as a wisp of smoke that manifested itself in front of the blue room, which had been a nursery.

The ghost's activity became much more intense and alarming in the summer of 2004, when Janet and her family were getting ready to move out of the old mansion. Events culminated when Janet's husband, Gary, came to the house one night to collect some things. The family had already moved out, so the place was dark and nearly empty. Gary planned to be in the house for only a short time. As he was gathering some towels, he distinctly heard a girl's voice say, "No, don't leave." This happened twice. Shaken, the man picked up the phone to call home when he noticed something utterly shocking— a couple of knives left out on the counter were slowly turning in his direction. Slamming down the phone, he left the house immediately.

Truly, Eastport is distinguished by the ways in which its phantoms bring to life the darkest aspects of its history. Key political and cultural events are encapsulated in chilling supernatural encounters, usually in the apparitions of the forlorn, the mad, and the condemned. As we leave the decaying, half-deserted island city, we cannot help looking back in wonder and in horror. For here, the past refuses to die.

9

The Gravedigger's Tale

Be advised not to read this chapter when you are alone, for a truer, more ghastly tale couldn't be told. It is arguably the most sensationally gruesome instance of supernatural horror imaginable. All our worst nightmares are laid out here—being buried alive, the dead coming back to life, a faceless figure in black, and a willpower emanating from the cold clay of the grave.

This story was relayed to me in one of the old homes located near the Bayview Cemetery in Machiasport, Maine, where the events took place in the early 1940s. My source heard it from the original, a man we'll call Jeremiah, who was the town-gravedigger's son. As Jeremiah delivered his tale, my source emphasized, it was clear that he still suffered deep scars from the incident that happened more than sixty years ago.

Jeremiah's father was a gravedigger by profession. He also liked to take a nip from the bottle once in a while, but who could blame him? In those days, a grave was dug by hand, a backbreaking job. It was also a particularly unpleasant one, for beyond all the obvious reasons, there are the mechanics of hand-digging a grave. You must be in the grave, and so being, inter yourself six feet in the earth before the job is done. Thus, there is always a lurking sense that you are digging your own grave. Back in the 1940s in Down East Maine, if light were needed, you would use an oil lantern, adding to the gothic, graveside setting in which you were center stage.

One spring, in the midst of mud season, a woman in Machiasport died. It was arranged that she would be buried next to her sister in the Bayview Cemetery. By all appearances, a better resting place couldn't be had. The little burial ground—or *boneyard*, to use the Yankee expression—is peaceful and quaint. Situated on a hillside, it overlooks Larrabee Cove and the islands of Machias Bay. Apple trees and a rock wall line one side of the cemetery. It's hard to believe that such a tranquil place could be the setting for one of the most ghastly of ghost stories, but truth is often stranger than fiction. Clearly, the world seen from the surface is but a pretty covering for the depths of dark rock and soil below.

On a cool, misty afternoon when the salty air hung heavy over the land, Jeremiah and his father headed to the site of the grave that needed digging. It was the day before the funeral was scheduled. They found the site directly next to the grave of Alice, the sister of the woman to be interred the next day. Since Alice had died twelve years before, she lay alone in the ground. Tomorrow morning, though, her sister would join her for a reunion lasting into eternity.

With hand shovels, father and son broke the sod next to the remains of Alice. The work of digging the new grave was hard going and took longer than expected. Even though the cemetery was well drained, the ground was wet and mucky because of the season. Then there were the many breaks taken by Jeremiah's father, as well as his frequent trips to the truck, where he kept his bottle. During these times, the task of digging fell to the boy, who did more than his share of the work by the end of the day.

Because it was misty, evening came quickly. As it crept through the cemetery, each of the white graves that lined the hillside began to fade and then disappear, one by one, into the blackness. His face sweaty and streaked with clay, Jeremiah looked anxiously in the direction of the truck, which he could barely see in the darkness. He considered calling out to his father, but decided against it; surely, he must be coming along soon. Like the darkness engulfing him, or the phantom wisps of ground fog encircling his feet, a dull uneasiness began to settle around Jeremiah. Finally, he saw a light appear and grow closer. The lantern his father carried was casting garish shadows over the man's weathered face as he loomed above his son. He thrust the lantern into his son's hand and crawled into the open grave where there was still a foot or more of earth to remove. Only the scraping of the spade and the sucking sound of wet earth broke the eerie silence. He finished the digging a short time later, never having spoken a word.

What happened next was totally unexpected. Jeremiah's father was on his knees inspecting the bottom of the grave to make sure it was perfectly level when the unthinkable happened. Owing perhaps to the wetness of the ground, one whole wall of dirt collapsed without warning. It buried Jeremiah's father up to his waist. But that was not why the man was screaming in wide-eyed, abject terror—he was not alone in the grave. In the dirt that caved in was a broken casket out of which fell the remains of Alice, the *sister* of the woman destined for the new grave. The skeleton had landed on Jeremiah's father, draping itself over the shoulders of the terrified man. The skull leered in a horrible parody of a smile. Still screaming, Jeremiah's father flung the skeleton back and clawed madly at the dirt, finally extricating himself. But as he scrambled out of the collapsed grave, he knocked over the oil lantern. Suddenly, he and his son and the skeleton of Alice were thrown into complete darkness.

The next thing Jeremiah knew, he was running in the direction of the truck, followed by his father, who had stopped to throw up. Clearly shaken, the man had no intention of going back to get his tools or to cover up the skeleton that had been exposed. Jumping into the truck, he turned it on and threw it into gear. There would be no going back now. The only thing to do was to arrive early the next morning and finish the job before the funeral. As the truck left the cemetery, Jeremiah's father tried his best to cover up the fear that had taken hold of him. In a gruff voice, he began blaming the boy for the cave-in, effectively sweeping his terror behind a wall of rage.

Terrible dreams ensued, no doubt, for both father and son, perhaps of Alice waking up to greet her sister in the cold of the grave. The nightmares were far from over when a pleasant spring morning ushered in the next day. Jeremiah and his father were doomed to rush back to the grave with its dread contents. Imagine their surprise when they arrived there and discovered that the skeleton had disappeared. In addition, the grave was cleaned out. There was no sign of the earlier cave-in. Cautiously, the gravedigger questioned his son as to the events from the night before. Clearly, the man wondered if he had imagined the wall collapsing and the skeleton draping itself around his shoulders. But to his dismay, his son confirmed all of his worst fears.

Jeremiah and his father waited for the funeral to end. The hearse had carried the body up the Port Road, and the mourners had assembled at the gravesite where the two sisters would finally rest side by side. Then, the short service concluded, and the black-clad people left the burial ground. Jeremiah and his father moved to the grave to shovel in the dirt. They were too busy to notice a solitary mourner watching them. For some time after everyone else had departed, a woman in black waited patiently in a corner of the cemetery. When the job was finished, and the mound of earth over the grave raked smoothly, Jeremiah and his father headed to their truck to load their gear.

The final horror came just as Jeremiah was leaving the cemetery. At this time, the lone mourner carefully picked her way through the cemetery and arrived at the site of the fresh grave. She was a well-dressed woman decked out completely in black. A large bonnet shielded her face, and a shawl hung loosely around her narrow shoulders. Standing in the middle of the otherwise empty cemetery, she looked ominous even in broad daylight. So it was no surprise that Jeremiah took one last look over his shoulder before he climbed into his father's truck.

Although the woman was staring directly at him, her face was hidden completely in the deep shadow of her bonnet. But the boy had no difficulty seeing her arm and her hand as she waved goodbye. There was nothing but old bones and sinews that glinted in the harsh sunlight. Jeremiah gasped, his mind wrenching in a horror that would haunt him for the rest of his days. It was not a living woman he saw, but a skeleton—none other than Alice! Her sisterly bonds outlived even the grave.

10

Ghosts of the Gables

Take an eighteenth-century Down East Maine sea-captain's house, add a secret room and a whole party of spirits, and the result is a recipe for the perfect ghost story. Indeed, the Gables of Machiasport is one of the most haunted homes in the region, giving rise to theories that it may be built over some kind of portal or opening to the spirit world. Most chilling of all is an unexplained death that took place here more than one hundred years ago. This mysterious event is the basis for the most celebrated legend of the house. Apparently, the spirit of a man who died at sea came home to claim the life of his grieving widow.

The two-hundred-year-old house sits perched on a ridge overlooking historic Machias Bay. The name of the home comes from two huge needle-peak gables that grace the oldest section of the house, which dates from the 1790s. In true Maine fashion, new sections, or ells, were added in the middle of the nineteenth century: thirteen rooms now make up the living quarters of the structure. A whole succession of sea captains and their families occupied the rambling house until the 1920s, when it was purchased by Dr. Francis Gano Benedict, a famous chemist and physiologist. When Dr. Teresa Amuso bought the house sixty years later, an elderly woman of Machiasport asked her if Dr. Benedict had yet made a visit. Teresa was shocked since the scientist had been dead since 1957. "Oh, that doesn't matter," the woman responded. "Dr. Benedict has been known to visit the house since he died in it."

Shortly after this encounter, Teresa and her son Paul were listening to a Mozart sonata when a truly strange incident occurred. In the middle of the classical piece, a jazz instrumental from the 1920s began playing and lasted for thirty or forty seconds. How this occurred remains a mystery because the only equipment being used was an old-fashioned record player. No defect could be found in the record, and when the sonata was replayed, the jazzy interval could not be found.

While no one seems to have seen the ghost of Dr. Benedict, the same cannot be said for the spirit of his wife. A carpenter working at the house, Scott Eebo, was not a believer in ghosts until he had his own unforgettable experience. He was refurbishing the servants' quarters and had just sat down for a break. Outside the low windows that looked over the back garden, he saw a gray-haired, matronly woman gliding through the yard. He stated that, "as she moved, it looked like all the vegetation she passed was withering away." Scott was quite shaken by the experience, particularly later when he was shown a picture of Mrs. Cornelia Golay Benedict, who died in 1961. "That's the same lady!" he cried out in horror.

Other supernatural occurrences create the impression that the house is populated by a veritable crowd of spirits. More than one guest has mentioned seeing a young man dressed in dark pants and a white, billowy shirt. He has been seen at the top of the front stairs and in a bedroom. Another time, three people were awakened in the middle of the night by the sounds of a woman singing one note over and over. Most common of all are the sounds of a party downstairs late at night. From darkened, empty rooms drift the distant sounds of voices, clinking glasses, and cabinet doors opening and closing. One of the most unusual spirits seen at the Gables is a ghost cat that appears sitting by a wall in the living room or else walking through that wall in the same place. When old floor plans of the house were found, it was discovered that an outside door was once located in exactly the place the ghost cat has appeared.

A possible murder points to the most legendary ghost of the Gables, a restless spirit that may have come from the dead to murder his widow. More than one hundred years ago, the house was owned by Charles Welch, a wealthy shipmaster. In 1893 he had been warned not to go to Brazil, but he went anyway, contracted yellow fever, and died before he could return home. Apparently, his spirit made the trip back: seven years after his death, on the evening of January 23, 1900, events took a terrifying turn. Amelia, the widow of Captain Welch, left the Gables early that evening, claiming she was going out to visit a friend. When their mother did not return, Amelia's two daughters and her son roused members of the community. As the hour grew late, an all-out alarm was issued; a large search party was formed by midnight.

The body of Amelia Welch was discovered at dawn the next day. It was lying on the seashore near the churchyard, which is at the bottom of the hill down from the Gables. Too all, it looked like Amelia had drowned, her body left on the beach by the receding tide. The coroner, however, discovered no water in the woman's lungs. Also her hair was dry. Technically, the forty-three-year-old woman had died of suffocation, apparently by strangulation. Wrapped around her neck was a veil that she hadn't worn when she left the house; in addition Amelia was found wearing a new coat, one she did not have on when she ventured out for the evening. One other detail was noted—Amelia went alone to the shore. This could be determined because of a fresh snowfall from the night before. The only footprints were her own, and they showed she had paced back and forth as if she were in torment. For the next few days, the newspapers ran articles with headlines debating murder or suicide and describing the panic that overtook Machiasport.

Although the investigation eventually came up with a theory of suicide, the family and many people in the community disagreed and suspected foul play, considering that "the woman was choked to death by some person unknown." Certainly, it would be hard to strangle oneself. And then, despite the death of her husband in 1893, Amelia was not a typical candidate for suicide. Not only was the woman wealthy, but she was also, in the words of the *Bangor Daily Commercial*, "one of the most highly respected women of this place. She has been in good health and her surroundings were of a nature to make suicide seem improbable."

Pressured to come up with an explanation, investigators eventually claimed that the woman had soaked the veil in chloroform and suffocated herself. While possibly true, this theory was merely conjecture based on the position of the body and the veil. Also sketchy was the motivation investigators proposed for suicide. On occasion Amelia had apparently stated that she thought she was going crazy, but, depending on the context, this might only be a figurative expression. Yet if the case for suicide seemed farfetched, so did the arguments for an accident or a murder. By their natures, all theories seemed particularly bizarre. Perhaps, then, the baffling case was best summed up by the statement made in the *Bangor Daily News* that there was "no reasonable explanation of the death of Mrs. Welch."

From the point of view of the supernatural, there is one stark possibility. Appearances indicate that Amelia had gone to meet the spirit of her husband on the night of January 23, 1900. After all, she had walked to the beach below the churchyard where the gravestones lined the snowy bluff; and there was the veil she took with her, which added both a bridal and a funereal quality to her attire. Most likely, then, "the friend" she was going to meet was none other than her dead husband. As if she planned to go on a journey, she was dressed in a new coat. The strange circumstances of her death indicate that she did indeed meet the spirit of her husband. Amelia appeared to have been alone, yet she may have been strangled. Is it possible that the ghost of Charles Welch took the life of his grieving widow? If ghosts can move objects and make other physical impressions, perhaps this is possible, however unthinkable.

One wonders how willingly Amelia departed this world. Was her grief so great that she wanted only to join her husband's spirit? Or was she the victim of a ghostly sea captain coming back to claim his ownership of her? The detail of her footprints on the shore is interesting in light of one other supernatural happening at the Gables. On stormy nights, the sound of footsteps could be distinctly heard from a secret room located on the second floor of the house. This room was once accessible only through the back of a closet in another bedroom. While no one stayed in the secret room, Teresa Amuso—who bought the Gables in the 1980s—often heard the sound of footsteps, as did her guests and family members on certain occasions. When the room was checked, it was always dark and empty. Perhaps it was the ghost of Amelia, who once paced the floor on stormy nights like she did along the beach on the night of her death. While the truth will never be known, the ghostly footsteps have not been heard since Amelia's story came to light.

The Gables continues to stand on its wooded ridge overlooking the Atlantic. Many of its previous occupants have reappeared over the years. Sometimes it has even seemed as if the dead are gathering for midnight revels, when the sounds of voices and of music carry through the dark and empty rooms. So many supernatural occurrences give rise to the impression that the house contains a portal to realms unknown. In any case, the Gables is home to one of the most chilling and mysterious of all ghost encounters—the taking of Amelia Welch.

I I

Bad Little Falls

Machias, the shire town of Washington County, gets its name from an Abnaki word loosely interpreted as meaning "bad little falls." Many residents and visitors alike assume the term refers to the dangers of the falls, which form a churning whirlpool that literally thunders throughout the town, especially during spring flooding of the Machias River. But the name bad little falls does not mean dangerous little falls. The closest literal translation is apparently "the little falls in the evil place." Although ancient artifacts turn up frequently in the area, none seem to have been discovered around the falls or on nearby College Hill, indicating that Native Americans shunned the place. Indeed, a history of tragedy and death lends credence to the sense that there is something evil about the place. In the whispered legends of the region, this presence is the source of many hauntings that plague the small community of Machias.

To begin with, the falls have been the watery grave for many a hapless individual. The most recent event happened to an educator in the

1990s, whose car slid on ice and fell into the falls. Although rescuers rushed immediately to her aid, the woman drowned before she could be retrieved. During the lumbering years there were undoubtedly many fatalities in or around the falls, the results of men trying to break up the deadly log jams that formed in the area. In a sledding accident in the 1870s, a boy slid out onto the frozen river and fell through the ice. His lifeless body was discovered caught on a log abutment supporting the covered bridge over the falls. On the same covered bridge during the War of 1812, a British soldier trying to defect was shot and killed, and for months his bloodstains on the wooden bridge were an object of terror for all passersby.

The University of Maine at Machias, perched on College Hill above the falls, is home to a number of phantoms and sinister legends. Over the years more than a hundred people have insisted that one of the dormitories, Dorward Hall, is haunted by restless spirits. Students complain of the sound of footsteps and voices in quarters of the building that are empty or being renovated. In one of the stairwells there is a face discernible on the wall—a face that is rumored to be the spirit of a student who was lost and forgotten in a crawlspace after everyone went home for the summer vacation one year. There are also legends that the dorm is haunted by the spirit of a serial killer who went on a murderous rampage before taking his own life. Another ghost is claimed to be the apparition of a girl who committed suicide by hanging herself from the dormitory's large balcony, which has since been closed. According to a tale circulated on late nights, the girl was led to take her own life as the result of a séance in which she was possessed by an evil spirit.

Supposedly, the dorm is also haunted by the apparitions of children and the spirit of a man who terrorizes them. Many students claim to have seen and heard the children. Jennie Dickens, for example, lived in Dorward Hall when she first came to Machias. During her freshman orientation, she was repeatedly awakened by the laughter of children. During the same period, students in the dorm were complaining that toys or stuffed animals they owned had been moved around during the night. Jennie and some other first-year students decided to use a Ouija board, and in her words "we were able to contact one of the children that night. He told us there were three children, a girl and two boys. They were kept here by the 'bad man' and could only sneak out for a little while before returning to 'hell.' " When the older students returned to the campus, Jennie and her friends discovered that the ghostly children have been making appearances for years and that "hell" is located in Dorward Hall. It refers to the bottom landing of one of the staircases.

In researching the history of Dorward Hall, I found nothing to support its most ghastly legends. Leaving aside the account of the ghosts of children, who supposedly died before the dormitory was built, there is no historical basis to the tragedies assigned to the place. For example, a student did not commit suicide in Dorward Hall by hanging herself from the balcony. According to the administration of the campus, the balcony is closed as a routine safety protocol. There is also no substantiation of a student having been accidentally walled up in the facility. And certainly the place has never been the scene of a serial-killer's bloodbath. The building is not particularly old, having been built in the early 1960s, and as far as I could learn, it was not constructed on the site of an older structure. (The location of the dormitory was once an overgrown horse pasture.) Perhaps, then, the source of some legends and ghostly activity predates the history of the institution. One cannot help wondering if the hauntings are attributable in some way to the evil of the falls nearby: Dorward, in fact, is the residence hall located closest to the falls. The gory legends would then be a way of putting a face on a nameless, malevolent force of ancient origin.

Dorward Hall is not the only building reputedly haunted. The Merrill Library has also been the setting for some strange encounters: One night, for instance, a worker was alone in the library, which was so quiet that she could hear a pin drop. An hour before closing, she made her customary rounds. Everything seemed to be in order, so she returned to the circulation desk to wait out her shift. During this time, no one came into the library. Later, when the worker was closing the library for the night, she discovered, to her horror, that all the books from a large shelf were lying scattered over the floor nearby. How this happened is anyone's guess; all the books had been in their place a short time before, and not a single sound was made, an impossible feat to accomplish given the deep silence reigning that night. Although Merrill Library is connected to Torrey Hall, where a student once died on the second floor, there is no historical explanation for the library being haunted. Since no tragic event took place there, we are left to wonder if there is something about the location or place that is, for lack of a better word, *bad*.

Even closer to the falls is an old house on Elm Street that has been subject to some horrifying instances of the supernatural. Candles have a way of blowing out and then relighting themselves. Doors open and then close on their own accord; once, they did this in succession, with each door opening in sequence. Ghostly activities seem concentrated on the 27th of every month. Steve Wierzbowski, who lives in the house, along with many others who have visited, including Evan Dodge, can attest to the nightly disturbances that have taken place there. Once, Steve placed a voice-activated tape recorder in an old second-floor office that seemed particularly riddled by ghostly activity. When the tape was replayed, there were strange, mumbling sounds on the recording. Steve slowed down the speed of the tape, and to his horror—and that of Evan, who was present at the time—heard an unearthly voice whisper over and over again, "I see you, Steve. Get out."

The area around the bad little falls is the subject of many ghost stories involving loggers doomed to return from the dead. A legend passed down in a local family concerns a man we'll call Lowell and his brother, both of whom worked the log drives on the Machias River near the falls. Syndell Parks interviewed a descendent of Lowell's who described the fateful afternoon when tragedy struck. "The sun was out and the birds sounded from all directions as the Roberts Family River Drive drove down the current. My grandfather and his brother were among many working on the boat." Up ahead, a logjam blocked progress, so "my grandfather's brother, being full of youthful vigor at the age of twenty one, went with a few good men to break up the jam. As they were working, the log supporting my grandfather's brother suddenly shifted, causing him to fall beneath the surface." The man was never seen alive again. Several weeks later, however, on a misty morning when Lowell was again working the river, he passed a small logjam close to the spot where his brother had drowned. As Lowell's descendent put it, "My grandfather stared into the dim mist, lost in his own thoughts. Out of the corner of his eye he caught a movement over the logs. He focused in on the movement and saw a shadowed figure. The figure was working on breaking up the logjam. He could hear the crackling of the pick on the wood and the snap of logs being forced to move. My grandfather, being so close to his late brother, knew that this was the same man."

Of all the stories involving ghostly loggers, one stands out as the most remarkable, for in this account a young man not only saw the apparitions of dead loggers, but also seems to have been transported momentarily back in time. The incident happened to Kenny Hoffman on an autumn night when the weather was unusual, being windy and foggy at the same time. Kenny had walked down College Hill and into the Bad Little Falls Park. Then his travels took him to an abandoned railroad track running along the river at the base of the falls. Even in the mist, from that spot he should have been able to see a good portion of Main Street, but as Kenny states, "When I looked up I couldn't see the usual sites, and I was thinking maybe it was just the fog or something." But this didn't explain the obstructions, for it seemed to Kenny as if shadowy buildings were blocking his view. Indeed, in the same location buildings had once stood when the waterfront was a busy shipping center, but these structures had long since disappeared.

Then, from out of the fog, Kenny noticed a bunch of logs floating down the river. He peered closer, and that's when he saw an apparition of a man. Kenny states that the figure was "riding the logs, and I saw him going along, using his pike to push apart the logs so they didn't jam up, and then soon enough another guy comes along right behind him doing the same thing. Well, between the two, a log jam formed up." Kenny watched in horror as the man in back tried to release the tangle. Suddenly, the log he was standing on turned, so the man tried to step onto another log, which also spun under his feet, causing him to lose his balance and fall into the river. At this moment, the man in front rushed to the other's aid only to drown when he, too, fell under the treacherous logs. Then, as Kenny put it, "the whole thing disappears, and the wind is still going, and I get this feeling that I'm not supposed to be there, that this was an accident that probably happened regularly, but that I was not supposed to have seen it." Quickly leaving, he was shaken by an experience that appeared to have been a journey back in time.

Before we take leave of the falls at Machias, we must make note of a local practice that contributes to their negative characterization: bad little falls are the perfect place to dispose of objects associated with pain and grief and bad luck. Like the opposite of a wishing well, the falls have become a place where residents bury all they might hope to forget. It is common for someone slighted in love to toss into the churning water a once-precious memento from a beloved. Accordingly, there is rumored to be a strange assortment of objects at the bottom of the falls, including engagement rings, lockets, and even a statue of the Indian god Shiva.

Whatever the true nature of the falls in Machias, there is no doubt that they are subject to tragedy and dark legends that go back hundreds if not thousands of years.

12

The Mask from Bali

Maine author Sarah Orne Jewett once pointed out that Maine was more isolated at the turn of the twentieth century than it was during the first half of the nineteenth century, when the coastline bustled with trade and travelers from all over the globe. There was, then, a cosmopolitan quality to the seaside hamlets that since has been lost and mostly forgotten. Contact with the far-flung places was sometimes sinister, planting the seed for many a ghost story involving exotic disease, ominous strangers, and unspeakable rituals. Although the following story took place recently, it evokes those bygone days. The mask from Bali that showed up in Machias one summer was apparently accompanied by a malevolent spirit that brings bad luck to all who own the object. In short, the mask from Bali is cursed.

This strange tale concerns a simple, carved wooden mask that is not particularly old. The mask depicts a skull. While this particular motif may be disturbing to some individuals, it does not make the mask unusual: there is an entire line of Balinese carvings with a theme of skeletons. The mask in question once hung in The Winter Ravens, a store on Water Street owned by Joanne Albee. Joanne purchased the mask from an import supplier in Trenton, Maine. One day, in early fall, a young man came into The Winter Ravens and bought the mask. Nothing seemed unusual at the time to Joanne; it would be later that she recognized all of the warning signs, the spiral of unfortunate events linked to the mask from Bali.

In all, Joanne had the mask for three months before selling it to the young man we'll call Trevor. During this time period, Joanne suffered through a relentless tide of misfortune, the worst of which concerned her health. By the time she sold the mask, she was liter-ally worried for her life. Having discovered a lump in her breast, Joanne had gone to local doctors who thought the tumor looked malignant and advised her to go to Bangor and have it examined. With her brother minding the store, Joanne set out a couple days later. While in Bangor, Joanne called to see how things were going. That was when she received startling news: Trevor had just been in the store and was visibly shaken and wanted to return the mask, claiming it was cursed. Joanne's brother informed Trevor that he would have to wait until the owner was back before the item could be returned.

Trevor went on to relay a tale of bad luck that began as soon as he had purchased the mask. As he was leaving the store with the skull mask still in its crisp paper bag, Trevor almost got into a car accident. If he hadn't swerved his car at just the right moment, he would have been killed, driven off the bridge on Dublin Street into the churning waterfalls from which Machias got its name.

With the mask still in his car, Trevor drove directly to work, where he suffered a most bizarre accident. He tripped and fell and landed directly on the top of his head, almost as if he were tipped and swiveled completely around. He couldn't have repeated the stunt if he had tried. With his head bruised and throbbing, and his shoulder feeling sprained, Trevor went home for the day. When he arrived at his house, he had another surprise. His dog, that he claims is the friendliest animal in the world, attacked him, growling, lunging, and even biting his owner in a completely unprecedented fashion. With all this having happened in the two hours since he bought the mask, Trevor decided it was cursed and vowed to return it. Besides, on closer inspection he noted something unsettling about the object, something that he couldn't put into words. A collector of masks, Trevor owned specimens from all over the world, many purchased by his uncle, an avid traveler. The mask from Bali, however, was different. It seemed much more than an object. Hovering around the artifact like an invisible shadow, there seemed to be a dark force or spirit.

As Joanne talked with her brother, she began to piece together all of the events that had occurred in her personal life since she acquired the mask the previous summer. Perhaps it was coincidence, but her troubles accompanied the arrival of that ominous mask. These troubles also seemed to depart with it. Since she sold the mask, her luck was changing. In Bangor, Joanne learned that the lump in her breast was a harmless cyst, but as she stated, "I had gotten rid of the mask by then." On the way back to Machias, Joanne's thoughts persistently returned to the mask from Bali. On impulse, she stopped in Trenton, where she originally bought the mask from an importer whom we'll refer to as Dianne. Joanne related the twisted tale of the mask, but the Trenton shopkeeper just laughed. Of course, a mask cannot be cursed!

Still intrigued, Joanne visited a mutual friend. When Joanne related the story of the mask, ending with the skeptical reception she had received in Trenton that day, her friend was shocked but not surprised. "Dianne shouldn't be laughing," Joanne's friend stated, "because she ought to think about what has happened to her since she had the mask." After a short, stunned silence on Joanne's part, she listened helplessly as the tale of the mask continued to enfold.

Dianne and her husband run an importing business and spend their winters in Bali. The year before, when they acquired the mask in question, nearly half of their shipment of products had been stolen. The desperate importers then hired a stranger to help them restock their merchandise. This man literally showed up on their doorstep in Bali, down on his luck. Sympathizing with his plight, Dianne and her husband hired him. When he delivered the new merchandise as promised, Dianne and her husband were pleased, but as they were getting ready to return to the United States, the stranger ran off, robbing them of more than $2,000 worth of jewelry.

Her head buzzing with all she had learned, Joanne continued home to Machias. The next day, Trevor brought the cursed mask, insisting he be able to return it. By now, Joanne was understandably reluctant to take it back into her possession. She could simply have reimbursed the young man and left him to dispose of the mask, but she thought otherwise. She later stated, "I debated whether or not I should take this mask back, but out of the kindness of my heart, I said okay."

Joanne decided to find out more about the mask. She discovered that in Bali the spirit world includes ghosts and demons as well as elemental entities like tree spirits that inhabit certain wood. Some Balinese masks are made with secret spells and rituals, but this does not apply to the masks carved for the retail market. Apparently, the cursed mask wasn't meant to be sold. Perhaps it was acquired through the stranger hired by Dianne and her husband to help them restock their stolen merchandise in Indonesia. Or maybe it was purchased by the importers themselves and was among the goods left behind after their first robbery. At any rate, the mask was back, and Joanne needed to do something about it.

Joanne hoped to find a way to lift the mask's curse, but its bad luck continued unabated. She learned of a young woman, a friend of Trevor's, who was also stricken from contact with the object. Apparently, before he returned the mask, Trevor had left it in her car, only informing her later when she came to him in tears about how her life "was suddenly going to hell." A few days after hearing this, Joanne discovered she herself was the victim of credit-card theft. Deciding that enough was enough, Joanne planned to throw the mask over the falls in Machias that night and "send it back to Bali." When she let one of her regular customers know of her intent, he begged her to give him the mask despite its awful reputation. She was reluctant until he promised to get rid of it at the very first sign of any trouble. Unfortunately, he didn't heed her warning. Shortly after he acquired the mask, his wife was diagnosed with multiple sclerosis, and she quickly began to decline. Even then, though, he refused to destroy the mask, keeping it hidden in the back of a closet.

Thus the cycle of misfortune continues, drawing more and more people into its downward spiral, and yet the skeleton mask persists in changing hands and avoiding destruction. Perhaps the mask not only brings bad luck, but also a strange, irrational attachment. Consequently, whatever spirit is associated with the mask continues to wreak its havoc all the way from Indonesia to Down East Maine.

13

The Haunted Portrait

Houses are known to have their ghosts. And so are certain locales or places. But can an object be haunted? What about a painting or a photograph? Indeed, who hasn't experienced the unsettling feeling that accompanies a portrait that follows you with its eyes? The following tale from Columbia, Maine, takes this eerie sensation to the utmost degree, for the portrait of a woman located in an old house is actually animated, possessed by the spirit of the original subject, Mary, a woman with the proverbial axe to grind.

When Loretta MacLeod moved into her house on the Epping Road, she didn't expect to find it inhabited. The house was built in 1863 and had stayed in the same family for one hundred and twenty years, so it contained all of the original furnishings as well as objects of sentimental value, such as letters and awards and baby clothes.

Apparently, when the Civil War broke out, the man who built the house went off to fight and was killed. Unable to support herself and her children, his wife had to sell the house. Shortly after the sale, however, the widow married the man who had purchased the house.

When Loretta MacLeod bought the home, among the original possessions was a portrait of a woman named Mary, who was the sister of the first husband, the man who built the house. The portrait of Mary hung at the end of a long first-floor hall, in a place central to the activity of the household.

For a long time Loretta didn't notice what was going on with the picture. This is no surprise considering her busy lifestyle: At the time, she and her husband had two small children, and she was pregnant with a third. The MacLeods also had adopted children; in addition, cousins and nieces and nephews were always around. Clearly, this wasn't a quiet, contemplative environment. Activity abounded, and with it, noises—from laughter and play to tantrums and arguments among children.

As her family grew in numbers, Loretta began to feel, in her words, "as if something was watching me or over the house." One day she noticed that the picture of Mary was changing. Loretta writes, "Her normal blank expression had taken on an angry look. I began to pay closer attention to Mary and realized that the noisier the house got, the more angry her expression. It was rarely a happy, serene-looking face anymore. The noisier my children became, the uglier the picture became. When the house was quiet, after the children were in bed, or were all outside for something, her expression would be back to normal."

Now, it's easy to read thoughts or emotions into images. In the same way we see figures in clouds, we can see a picture in a completely different light, depending on our mood or sensitivity at the time. But in the case of Mary's portrait, there could be no doubt that her changing expressions were supernatural, not mere tricks of the eye or the mind. Mary's expression would change in very dramatic ways. Loretta writes that "Many times she would frown so hard at me that I would be forced to look over at her to see what she was doing."

Intrigued at first, Loretta did more research and discovered that Mary never lived in the house or, apparently, even visited it. A well-to-do woman, Mary lived in Michigan, where she was married but childless. While we'll never know for sure, we can surmise that Mary never visited because she didn't like children. Nonetheless, her portrait had been in the house for many years. From the early 1940s until Loretta bought it, the house was occupied only during the blueberry season in July and August. Thus, Loretta reckoned that the home must have been very quiet and tranquil for most of the year. The transition, then, to Loretta's busy family life must have come as quite a shock to the high-strung spirit.

Eventually, Loretta began to grow uneasy with the portrait. Its shifting, angry expressions might have been interesting at first, but they became disturbing as time wore on. Besides, the picture was clearly targeting her children, responding to them in negative ways, which bothered Loretta. So she finally took the portrait down and moved it into the woodshed. When this was done, Mary began to manifest herself through the more conventional means of the spirit world—objects would be missing or would turn up in strange and unusual places. These events were small, even trivial in themselves, but they spoke volumes about Mary's continued presence.

For example, once Loretta was carrying wood into the house. She was alone, and the wood was located in the shed where the portrait of Mary hung. To keep the door open, Loretta propped it with a bucket; however, when she came back for her second armload, the shed door was closed. Loretta writes, "It could have slid shut, and the bucket pushed forward, so I paid no attention to it, just put the bucket back." A few minutes later, returning for a third load of wood, Loretta found the door closed again, but this time the bucket had been placed behind the door. There were no animals in the area, and there was no way to explain how the bucket could slide backwards and end up behind the door.

Loretta states that "Over the next few years, other circumstances around the house led me to believe that Mary was still around." But what could have accounted for these new kinds of manifestations? Perhaps Mary shifted things around because her portrait had been moved, tampering with her original venue or means of expression. Or perhaps she was insulted because she was resigned to the woodshed, despite the fact that it was relatively quiet. Or maybe Mary simply wanted to make her presence felt. We'll never know.

The baffling case of the haunted painting, singular as it is, has at least one parallel in the ghost tales of the region. In a store in Machias, hanging over a fireplace, there used to be a painting of a sea captain. When the store closed, the building was sold to a family who took down the portrait and placed it in the attic. The house changed hands again, and the new family liked the portrait even less than the previous owners did. In short, the painting was put out at the side of the road with the trash one day. Oddly, although the trash was removed, the portrait returned to the side of the house a few days later. Thinking that there had been a mistake and the portrait hadn't been picked up with the trash, the family tried again and again to throw out the painting. Each time it would reappear beside the house. Eventually, the owners gave up and hung the portrait of the sea captain back over the mantle where it presumably belonged. When this was accomplished, the home's occupants never again had trouble with the painting.

What can we conclude from these strange tales? Perhaps the portraits—especially Mary's—possessed what the Micmac Indians knew as the Power, which they defined as shape-shifting. For reasons that are inexplicable, the portrait of Mary could be an object imbued with the Power—power to manifest change, especially during times of heightened energy and activity. Of course, to societies steeped in magic and mysticism, photographs have always been suspected of stealing the soul. The same goes for paintings. In Judeo-Christian teachings, for example, paintings and carvings are essentially problematic, as seen, for example, in the biblical commandment "Thou shalt not make unto thee any graven image."

What bearing these issues have on the portrait of Mary and the painting of the sea captain is not clear, but the secret may lie in the very words we use to describe portraits that are especially well executed. That's when we praise the artist or photographer for having *captured* the *essence* or *spirit* of the subject.

14

On Pins and Needles

Certainly, manifestations of spirits can take many shapes and forms. Some ghosts appear only as a sense of smell, apparitions that conjure the scent of a perfume associated with a deceased loved one. Or sounds can be a ghost's primary mode of operation, heard as voices, music, or footsteps. But among the most bizarre and disturbing manifestations are the incidents that besieged a small household in Milbridge, Maine. Here the keynote of ghostly activity involved sharp objects—anything that could cut or puncture. Through a series of unexplainable events, two local educators confronted the full brunt of the supernatural.

The events occurred in the home of Brittany Ray and Ron Smith. The white house, located on a hill overlooking fields and the ocean, had been in Brittany's family for generations. While sharp objects were the primary targets of ghostly activity, there were other creepy happenings. Once, Brittany felt Ron come up behind her and put his hand on her shoulder, but when she turned around, no one was there. Another time, her father was cleaning out a shed on the property. He was hauling off old pictures and chairs, when suddenly, in a cabinet he hadn't opened, a music box from Christmas started to play. These incidents were weird, but they were the exception, not the norm, for a spirit with a fetish for the exceptionally sharp.

A whole set of incidents involved pins. One day, for example, around Labor Day, when school was just starting, Ron took out a new dress shirt and removed the straight pins, tossing them on a piece of furniture nearby. When he returned to the house later that day, he and Brittany were surprised. She states that "the pins were all sticking in the top of a flat round candle, lightly, and we didn't do it. It wasn't anything threatening. It was just there." On another occasion, while in the upstairs bathroom, Brittany had sewn a button onto an article of clothing, and she had tossed the thread and needle on the back of the toilet, where there was a bar of soap. She left for a few moments, and when she stepped back into the room, the needle was standing up in the soap. At the time of these events, Brittany and Ron had no children and were living in the house by themselves, so no one else could have been responsible for moving the pins or the needle.

The most startling of all events involved simple household scissors. Brittany came home one day in August and found the scissors she had left out on the countertop—scissors that were now standing straight up and balanced on a single point. The hard, smooth surface of the countertop prevented the scissors from being stuck into the material. Besides, not a mark was left from the scissors. This strange event happened three or four times for Brittany and once for Ron during the height of supernatural activity in the home. If the scissors were left out, they would be found later, standing on one sharp end. As soon as the scissors were touched, they fell. Brittany and Ron were left speechless.

The mystery had deepened. It was no longer a question of who or what was doing this, but *how* it was being done. Brittany and Ron tried repeatedly to balance the scissors, but the couple was never able to stand them up on one end without embedding that point in a soft material, like pine. On the Formica countertop, this feat was impossible to recreate. Brittany admitted that the "scissors incident spooked me. It was freaky, and I didn't know if we were going to stay." Something about the angle of the scissors also struck Brittany as totally alien, completely beyond the realm of possibility, thus unsettling in a frightening way.

Because of the sharp-object incidents, life at the Milbridge home began to change. Every pin or tack had to be accounted for; leaving them out became unthinkable. Someone gave the couple a holder for their scissors. Knives had to be used, then quickly put away, so they wouldn't be found later balanced on the nearest surface. As soon as Brittany and Ron cut food, they had to rush over to the kitchen sink and wash the knives and put them away. If the utensils were left in the sink, they might be found later, standing on their tips on the impenetrable countertop.

Events came to the boiling point a few months later. On a night in early November, the couple headed up to bed, shutting their bedroom door. Brittany was sleeping by the window when she woke up suddenly, as if someone had roused her. Her first thought was that her mother was in the room, even though the woman did not live with them. When Brittany went into the hallway, she realized that the house was burning hot. "You couldn't touch the railings—it was like fire. At the bottom of the stairs, our cat was on his back, belly out, legs out, panting. I went down, but it was hard to go down, it was so hot." The furnace had malfunctioned and was racing uncontrollably.

If Brittany hadn't awakened, it might have exploded and burned down the house. But why did she wake up? Because she and Ron had shut the bedroom door, the room was quiet and comfortable, not burning hot like the rest of the house.

The incident with the furnace calls into question the motivation behind the ghostly activities in the house. Brittany felt she had been assisted, roused to save herself and her household. Prior to this, she felt that the sharp-object incidents were becoming distinctly horrifying. But was Brittany's sense of security well founded? It all depends on what actually happened to the furnace and on what woke her up that fateful night. Brittany may have mistaken whatever spirit inhabited the house for her mother; in that case, the spirit was not a threat but a protector. Perhaps, however, it was the other way around, and a protective spirit was trying to intervene in a malicious-ghost's deadly chain of events.

Over and over, in a maddening way, the question comes up. Why would ghostly activity concern itself almost exclusively with sharp objects? One possibility is a ghost with a fetish or phobia for the very sharp. Some research supports this possibility. Long after the sharp-object incidents, the couple discovered that an ancestor of Brittany's was inordinately afraid of all things sharp. This woman had previously lived in the house, and Brittany's grandfather feels that the spirit of this woman still inhabits the place. He has been a firm believer in the supernatural ever since he went to a medium as a young man, after a couple he knew went to sea in a rowboat and never returned. The psychic told him about the accident and said that the woman's body would never be found, but that he would find the man's corpse on the back side of an island, and that the body would be face down. The friend's body was found exactly as described.

Brittany's grandfather will not enter one room in the Milbridge house, which he considers haunted. A caretaker who worked for the family saw the apparition of a woman in the window of that particular room. Could this be the woman who was afraid of sharp objects? The apparition appeared more than once during the time when the house was still empty, before Brittany and Ron moved in. There is another angle. Just after the height of activity in the house, Brittany discovered she was pregnant with her first child. Could the sharp-object incidents be somehow connected? Brittany wondered if the spirit in the house was trying to protect her by not letting her leave out potentially dangerous items. While this may be true, it doesn't address the unsettling, even threatening, nature of the experiences—their obsessive focus on objects that can inflict injury. Whatever the case may be, the spirit manifestations settled down in the house soon after Brittany gave birth to her daughter.

There is one more twist to the story of the spirit who manifested itself in the Milbridge home. According to Brittany, sharp-object incidents were escalating in the house shortly before the furnace malfunctioned. Perhaps there was a connection. Surely, pointed or sharp instruments are located in the mechanism of a furnace. Did the ghost manipulate these, like it did the pins, the needles, the knives, and the scissors? In this case, its probable intention was a potentially deadly "accident." We can only wonder how far this ghost would go to make its point.

15

Dead Lights and Luminous Ghosts

It is one o'clock in the morning in the middle of a Maine winter. The full moon glimmers on the waters of the North Atlantic and casts a lighted pathway across the oozing mudflats of low tide. Near the flats, a fisherman and his companion wait quietly in a small boat. Then they see what they have come for. It starts out as a green light hovering ten feet above the water, approximately one hundred feet from the boat. Shortly after it appears, the light plunges into the sea. Moments later it resurfaces with another green light. The two lights, moving together, almost look like glowing green eyes. When the fishermen try to move closer, the two lights dodge under the waves, then reappear three hundred yards away at the edge of the bay.

This incident, which occurred near Sullivan, Maine, in 2000, was gathered for me by Brian Simpson, who went on to say that the two men "sat in the boat for a few minutes completely terrified of course." Apparently, when the moon was right, the lights appeared like clockwork.

The account belongs to the most mysterious kind of supernatural sighting in the Down East region. Strange orbs of light, or *dead lights*, to borrow a phrase from author Stephen King, have been observed here for hundreds, maybe thousands, of years. They are recorded in the oral cultures of both Native Americans and English settlers. The Federal Aviation Administration has studied the lights, and so has the National Oceanic and Atmospheric Administration. Experts have been consulted—the state geologist from the Maine Geological Survey, the Maine state climatologist, as well as the science operations officer at the National Weather Service. These individuals and agencies have ruled out naturally occurring phenomena like phosphorescent gas, ball lightning, and earth lights—the latter produced by seismic action on quartz. So in the end, the mysterious spheres remain a testimony to an unsolved mystery, which lends its own kind of horror to their appearance.

Consider another incident involving these strange lights. They made the front page in the *Machias Valley News Observer* in July 2001, after a summer resident named Bonnie Thompson encountered them. The incident happened in the predawn hours of July 4 at Bonnie's secluded cottage in Addison. Awakened by her cat, Bonnie "stirred enough to catch a glimpse of light darting past her window." Curious, she got up and went to the window and observed approximately twenty glowing white orbs of light the size of basketballs. They hovered in her yard and darted among the trees only fifty feet from the house. Mesmerized, Bonnie watched the lights for nearly thirty minutes before they left the yard in "obvious teams of threes and fours." Bonnie later stated that "It sounds cool, and in the daylight it would be cool, but in the dark it was terrifying."

Drawn by the attention given the incident, other residents from

Down East reported strange lights they had seen over the years, not just in Addison, but in areas such as the Machias River Valley and the blueberry barrens along Route 191 heading toward Canada. At first no one claimed to have seen the orbs of light on the night of July 4. Then, three weeks after the incident, two other eyewitnesses came forward—Roz Roberts, another summer resident of Addison, and her ten-year-old son, Kevin. Around midnight on the Fourth, Kevin called to his mother to look out the window and see the "spooky-looking visitors."

Roz stated, "I thought he was just joking around at first," but when he persisted, she finally looked out the window and was shocked to witness balls of light darting about her yard—the same lights seen by Bonnie Thompson just a few hours later. Roz went on to say that "she was absolutely petrified but at the same time mesmerized, and watched until they all disappeared over the treetops." In a typical pattern, experts who were consulted were unable to explain the strange lights that appeared in Addison on the Fourth of July.

To this day, phantom lights remain a mystery to science; thus they figure prominently in the folklore of the region. Certainly, some residents associate these lights with stories of UFOs and, more frequently, to secret tests conducted by the government. Perhaps it is no accident that the remote, coastal area hosts top-secret facilities like Cutler Naval Base and an Air Force over-the-horizon radar installation in Columbia Falls. But there are also ancient traditions claiming that these strange lights are the restless spirits of the dead.

In one very old Down East legend, the dead lights are linked to Satan himself. They may be found in the Devil's Oven, a cave located on the tidal stretches of the Machias River. People claimed to have gone there on stormy nights, said Captain Nelson Proctor nearly fifty years ago, and "seen balls of fire darting all around the cave, inside and out, with screams that would make your hair curl." Proctor went on to state, "There have been so many weird tales about it, that the fishermen even give it wide berth. Tradition has it that some of the natives have heard old Satan himself calling for his worshippers to come into the cave and dine with him." The location of the Devil's Oven is intriguing because in recent decades there have been numerous sightings of strange lights—usually blue flashing orbs—on or around the Machias River, sometimes even traveling under the water.

If we dig deeper into the region's folklore, we find Native American accounts of luminous ghosts. Usually, these are presented as distinctly threatening. For example, there is the being known to the Micmacs as *skadegamutc*, a spirit that takes on various forms, including luminescent mist. The Malecites describe a spirit that is a dread messenger of death and whose name, *esquedewit*, means "fiery one." In a famous Malecite ghost tale, a hunter is chased by a spirit that leaves the corpse of a vampire and takes the form of a ball of light. Followed by the glowing apparition, the hunter runs to his village, screaming for help, receiving it only when arrows are shot into the ball of fire, finally driving it away.

Indeed, worldwide, there are accounts of ghosts that appear as glowing spheres of light. Consider the apparition of an angel descending in a ray of light or emerging from a ball of light. On a more ominous note, there are the infamous *corpse candles* of British and Scottish legend. Like the *cairn fires* of Icelandic tradition, these glowing lights are seen most often in forests and burial grounds and are thought to be spirits shut out of both heaven and hell, condemned to wander the earth for eternity. These luminous ghosts usually appear as white, gray, or black, but also exhibit other colors, including blue. They were considered unlucky in many cultures. The Romans called them the *ignis fatuus*, or "foolish fire." Darting around elusively, they lured travelers into the woods, where they would become lost. Today, orbs of light are the most documented anomaly in spirit photography.

Another kind of luminous ghost is the will-o'-the-wisp, which has a menacing tradition in the coastal wilds of Maine. The true will-o'-the-wisp is a glowing mist that can hover, depart, or follow on its own volition. Long believed to be an omen of death, the will-o'-the-wisp has often been mistaken for phosphorescent swamp gas. Like the orb of light, this elusive spirit shows itself in different colors. In the 1920s it appeared in the middle of Jonesboro. Known as the *green galoo*, the glowing mist crept from the Pleasant River and engulfed a nearby cemetery. Whether it is seen on land or water, the will-o'-the-wisp always brings with it a dread premonition.

Fred Watts, from Jonesboro, tells of a time years ago when his great aunt was very ill; one evening "the men of her household were aboard their fishing vessel" and the will-o'-the-wisp appeared, settling around the mast. When it landed on the deck, one brother cried out that his sister was dead, which turned out to be true. Anecdotes like these pepper the legends of the place.

No doubt, the deepest source of horror is the unknown, and nothing could be farther from human knowledge than the dead lights of Down East. Their strangeness adds to the yawning abyss of the unknown connected with ghosts in general. To be sure, we cannot ignore the long traditions regarding luminous ghosts. In the supernatural lore of the region, ghost lights have a place darkened by mystery and, in some cases, evil.

16

The Robinson House

Once described in *Down East* magazine as "one of the most spectacular empty homes in the state," the Robinson House stood for all that was supernatural in the region. A more haunted, remote, and lonely place would be difficult to find, yet the home sat on Main Street in East Machias, near the municipal building and the post office. The abandoned house was Victorian in style with a curving mansard roof built by ship-wrights back in the sailing days. Elaborate cornices and moldings graced the weather-beaten structure whose faded paint was the color of an old bone. Shades were drawn in many of the windows, but dark interior regions were visible through cracks and rips in the coverings. A brooding sense of the spirit world hung over the place, striking even the most casual passerby. A ghostly reminder of super-natural realms in the very heart of the everyday world, the Robinson House lived up to its appearance as the quintessential haunted house.

What is it about abandoned houses that make them appear haunted? Certainly, appearances play a part in structures that grow dilapidated and, thus, stand as testimony to loss and decay. This was no doubt the case with the once stately Robinson House that had become, in the words of one local resident, "a forbidding presence across from the old Aubrey Dwelley store." But abandoned houses are also mysterious by nature. We can't help but wondering why no one can occupy them for any length of time. This question certainly applied to the Robinson House, which stood empty for so long before being sold and briefly inhabited in the late 1990s. Its last owners did not stay long enough to recoup their losses. Rumors spread that no one could live in the house because it was troubled by restless spirits.

Perhaps the real reason why empty houses seem to be haunted is that they take on a life of their own. Amplified by the silence and emptiness, traces of the past intensify, growing unhampered like the dust in them that settles without disturbance. This was particularly the case in the Robinson House, which contained the remnants of its past. The family furnishings were all there, including a harpsichord in the parlor and pictures of ancestors hanging on the walls.

"Many believe that the house of the late Curville Robinson, which has been a prominent part of East Machias for nearly a century, was plagued by ghosts," states Gillian Gaddis, a resident of the town. Her aunt, Andrea Padilla, agrees. A caretaker for the house in the 1980s, Andrea and her daughter, Crystal, who was Gillian's age, spent a lot of time in the Robinson House. Andrea states that "The house was funny. It either likes you, or it doesn't. If it doesn't, look out." Apparently, the house had a strong dislike for Andrea's daughter. Gillian writes, "Whenever Crystal entered, the 'feel' of the house would become chilly, even on the warmest of days. Deep within the house, doors would begin to slam, hard enough to reverberate throughout all the rooms. Photographs and pictures would suddenly fall from the walls, the glass from their frames tinkling across the floors." Gillian had a taste of this experience. Once, as she and two friends were leaving the otherwise uninhabited house, a door upstairs slammed so hard that the whole building shook. Gillian claimed that she and her friends beat a hasty retreat.

Andrea's daughter had one particularly frightening experience in the house that hated her. It took place in an upstairs bedroom just after Crystal discovered a dusty antique toy, which had been lost underneath a drawer in a built-in dresser. At the very moment that she made this discovery, the door of the bedroom, which was wide open, slammed shut. There were no drafts in the house; it was securely sealed by its old-fashioned storm windows and storm doors. Startled already, the girl tried to leave the room only to discover that she was locked in. Using all her strength, she tried to budge the door, but to no avail, so she screamed for her mother. Andrea, who was in the attic, rushed down to see what was wrong. The woman states that she didn't even have to turn the doorknob to open the door. As soon as she touched the knob, the door sprang open on its own, in a way she hadn't seen before and wouldn't see again.

On more than one occasion, the ghosts of former occupants have made an appearance, particularly the specters of those who died trag- ically or mysteriously. Gillian writes, "Many people with whom I'm acquainted speak of actually seeing ghosts there." One relative of hers saw the apparition of a baby at the bottom of the house's front staircase. The same ghost also appeared in the kitchen. Apparently, this was the spirit of Henry Robinson, an infant who died in the house and was buried on the property. Another spirit may have dwelled in the dark, musty basement of the old structure. According to Andrea and Gillian, long ago, a Robinson man tumbled down the cellar stairs to his death. Rumor had it that he had been pushed. In the dining room was a mirror in which a ghost regularly appeared. Andrea states, "In the old, beveled mirror, you would always see something behind you, a vaporous figure. Some thought it was a woman; others thought it was a man."

Like many haunted dwellings, the Robinson House was subject to sudden temperature changes, which in this case were concentrated in an upstairs nursery. Containing a tiny iron bed and sloping walls covered with faded wallpaper, the room was located at the top of the front stairs, just off the old master bedroom. The atmosphere in the nursery was particularly charged. Even during the dog days of summer, a deep, penetrating chill hung over the room. Perhaps it was linked to the legend that the nursery was unhealthy or even dangerous: anyone who spent too much time in the room would inevitably become sick. "Speculation concerning the death of the infant Henry Robinson," writes Gillian, "includes the fact that his nursery was located in that same room."

Even the grounds of the Robinson House had a ghostly character. Tall grass and raspberry bushes grew up to the foundation, and the spires of fir trees darkened the background. While the house was not far from the road, the property stretched back for over a hundred fifty acres of wilderness. Children were often spooked by strange and unaccountable noises whenever they ventured too close to the empty house. Some residents of the town felt like they were being watched by something malevolent hidden inside the home.

In 2000 the Robinson House was torn down. Whether an unfortunate event or a blessing in disguise, a landmark had disappeared. Yet the house lives on through its many architectural pieces that were salvaged: the chandelier, some of the fancy moldings, fireplaces, and floors are now integrated into other structures in the community. Water from the "boiling spring" located on the Robinson property still serves several households in the village. But most of all, the house perpetuates itself through the ghost lore of Down East Maine. The place stands out as the epitome of the haunted house. Its secrets may be lost to time, but its legacy is still with us, brooding over a town, and pointing to the thinness of the veil between the living and the dead. Gone but not forgotten, the Robinson House has become its own kind of ghost.

17

The Devil Down East

pparently, the devil has a penchant for Down East
Maine. Writing during the time of the Salem Witch
Trials, Cotton Mather referred to the province of Maine
as the devil's country. Certainly, Mather was thinking of the vast,
isolated landscape and the shadowy forests where Satan could hide.
No doubt, he was also thinking of what he called the heathenish
practices of Indian savages. But his real point had to do with the
perceived backwardness of the area, the fact that it hosted few forms
of industry or urbanization. To a Puritan like Mather, this was one
sign that the devil held more sway here than he did in Massachu-
setts Bay, which God favored with prosperity as early as the first half
of the seventeenth century.

Today, Mather's claims seem not only bigoted but ridiculous. Yet
we should not dismiss them wholesale, for a dark legacy of the devil
does indeed hang over the land. Maine has changed a lot since the
time of the witch hunts, but the least-altered part of it is arguably
the lost coastline in the easternmost corner of the state. In this

remote, sparsely settled area, the marks of the devil run through cycles of whispered legend and find their place in regions of horror carved out far from prying eyes.

One of Down East's oldest English-based customs testifies to the proximity of Satan and involves children's shoes. It's not uncommon to hear of someone finding an antique shoe—especially a child's shoe—in the walls of an old house being renovated. Even the Burnham Tavern in Machias, the oldest building in eastern Maine and a historic site of the American Revolution, has had such a secret tucked away in its walls. The reason behind this quaint custom is intriguing. The idea is that a child's shoe placed in the walls will kick out the devil should he enter the house.

Other old tales of the region tell of the devil appearing in places associated with loose morals. The Prince of Darkness seemed to be fond of crashing parties. In an interview with a local resident, Jessica Brainerd and Rebecca Colson collected a strange tale in which the devil visited a dance hall in Lubec. The story took place in the 1940s at a place called the Twin Spruces, which hosted large dances every Saturday night. One evening a tall, dark stranger showed up. Someone happened to glance down at his feet, then screamed "Oh, my God, it's the devil!" As the tale goes, in place of feet, the man had cloven hooves. As Jessica and Rebecca's informant put it, "The guy vanished, and so did the people. Closed the dance down and never had another dance. It was in the paper—devil in dance hall." Another longtime resident of the area stated, "My mother wouldn't even let us kids walk past there." Apparently, the dance hall, which has recently reopened, once had a lurid reputation as a place where "all the maidens lost their virginity."

If we go back in time to the turn of the twentieth century and move to the little fishing hamlet of Bucks Harbor, we find the devil appearing in another dance hall. Nearly fifty years ago, Angelia Clark stated, "I have heard my mother-in-law tell of her experience with the devil in the dance hall many times. She claimed that the devil came to her in the form of heavy chains that fell about her feet. She ran in fright from the hall, but the chains followed her some distance, rattling and clanging at her heels." As in Lubec, the devil's appearance confirms certain Puritanical views. Angelia states, "many people in the little community . . . believed that dancing was very wicked and that the devil was in every dancehall."

Conjuring spirits was another way to invite in the devil. In one local account, a number of fishermen conducted an impromptu séance on Roque Island in the first half of the twentieth century. While they were drinking, it seems that they decided to call up other kinds of spirits. According to Mrs. Oscar Dunbar, who knew the men involved, "They placed their hands on the table, each joining another, making a complete circle. Someone suggested that they call up F.S. (a man who had been a wit and a heavy drinker all his life). They called out, 'We want F.S. . . .' There was a bottle of liquor on the shelf near the men, with the cork out, when they called his name, that bottle upset and the liquor ran out onto the floor, and on the table was tapped out in perfect rhythm 'The Devil's Horn Pipe.' "

Then, of course, there are tales of the devil arriving to collect the souls of sinners. These stories tell of a mysterious phantom in black who appears just hours before someone is about to die, supposedly to take the soul due him. His appearance never fails to strike terror in all who encounter him.

A Maine legend in this vein originated on Machias Bay. One stormy night, a man was lying in a terrible fever. His friends and relatives had gathered around him and expected him to pass away at any moment. They also thought his sickness was a punishment for his evil deeds. As the evening wore on, the attendants dropped to sleep, one by one; but in the middle of the night, they were awakened by the door banging in the wind. Then they noticed that the sick man had vanished! As Leona Roberts puts it, "Outside the rain had stopped. The man's footprints were visible. They led from Long Point into the bay, but they did not stop there. The prints came out of the water on the Cutler side and then became indistinct. Nor did the man walk alone. The devil walked with him. The footprints are still distinct today, many years later. The rocks have hardened to preserve them."

Prior to contact with Europeans, the Native Americans in the region did not have any figure corresponding to the devil in their folklore and belief systems, which were nonetheless peopled with witches, evil magicians, huge serpents, and demons. One of the most horrifying demons from Passamaquoddy tradition is the *chenoo* or *kewahqu'*. This haggard, wraithlike creature comes down from the far north. Its heart is made of ice, and it is a cannibal, even resorting to gnawing off its own flesh. The female chenoo is considered far more fierce and terrifying than the male. Her screaming cry, which sounds like that of a mountain lion, can cause madness, even death, for the listener. Imagine the horror of a woman, in a Passamaquoddy tale, who is gathering wood and stumbles onto the hungry demon leering at her with blazing eyes only inches away from her face. In one *chenoo* tale influenced by Christianity, the demon is driven away from a village when the people make crosses on the trees where they expect him to pass.

The devil doesn't crop up just in stories and customs of a moralizing nature; he also appears in secret places devoted to his worship. Carefully hidden throughout the area are a number of what appear to be satanic churches. Most of these sites are clearly the product of local teenagers spray-painting demonic symbols in remote places suitable for underage drinking. But there is still a deeply disturbing quality to some of these sites. For example, Machiasport's abandoned East Side Church, once nestled on the seashore, was desecrated and turned into a satanic altar. The building has since been demolished. Another secret church, hidden over the churning "bad little falls" of Machias, was located, ironically, under a small, picturesque park. On Howard Mountain in Bucks Harbor there used to be an abandoned radar installation that teens had covered with satanic inscriptions. No one could visit the place without feeling ill at ease; some people reported finding articles that seemed to belong to victims, such as a child's homework blowing around the place, or a woman's purse half buried in the mulch. Worst of all is a horror hidden in the hills near the dump in East Machias. An avid hunter out one fall day looking for game stumbled upon a strange path. It was cut like a switchback in a copse of firs, so that its opening was virtually invisible. The path led to a small, perfectly circular clearing amid a very dark and dense wood. Nailed to the trunks of the trees that formed the circle were the bleached skulls of animals. Below these skulls were small piles of bones, evidently from the carcasses remaining after the skulls had been nailed to the trees.

The preponderance of devilish legends from Down East gives us pause for reflection. Certainly, a Satanic legacy seems to enshroud this place, but what is its cause? Are these stories the nightmarish product of Puritanism? Are they forms of mass hallucination as in the case of the devil appearing in the middle of a crowded dancehall? Or is there *something* about the land—its remote and uncharted places—that lends itself to terror and dread messengers from infernal regions? At the very least, we're left with a frightening set of images: the shadowy stranger in the forest, the black-clad phantom at the deathbed, the bleached remains of unspeakable rituals, and the cannibalistic demon with madness gleaming in his eyes.

18

A Room Without Walls

In Harrington, Maine, stands a building shrouded with an air of immutable mystery and supernatural horror. Once a farmhouse—now a health center—the white structure with its rambling additions sits back off of Route 1. The place has been the setting of numerous hauntings and inexplicable occurrences, but what stands out the most is the experience of crossing over into totally different realms of space and time. In this sense, the house offers a terrifying glimpse into the heart of all hauntings.

Long before the old building was converted into the present-day health facility, it was rented as a two-family home. Greg Williams, a librarian in Machias, told me a chilling account concerning a friend of his, a student whom we'll refer to as Jason. Having lived twelve years in the house in Harrington, Jason was well acquainted with its supernatural dimensions. One day, for example, he had just returned from school. Kicking off his shoes, he sat down in the kitchen to do his homework. No one else was in the house, and a silence reigned as it can do only in the winter, when the leaves have fallen and the songbirds have fled south. Jason was unexpectedly startled from his studies by the sound of someone coming up behind him. As he swiveled around and saw that no one was there, he heard his name called softly but audibly, "Jasonnnnn." The boy was so frightened that he ran outside in his bare feet. Fortunately, his father had just pulled into the driveway, and the boy felt safe enough to go back inside the creepy structure.

The most terrifying and mind-boggling experience occurred in the old root cellar of the place. This room was very small, not much bigger than a large closet. It was also quite dark, without electricity and lighted by only one narrow window. Jason's mother kept potatoes in the root cellar, so on occasion he would have to go down there to retrieve some for her. Jason never liked the room because it was dark and creepy, but he had no reason to abhor it until one fateful evening. There was nothing unusual to begin with, no presentiment or warning of danger. Having been sent for potatoes, he headed down to the root cellar, where the last of the day's light filtered through the dust and the cobwebs caked on the window. Jason had just finished his task and was preparing to go back upstairs when he abruptly lost all sense of bearing. For some reason, the room had suddenly become completely black, darker than midnight.

Standing in the total darkness, the boy tried to fight back the panic rising inside him. In vain, he looked for the window, but it was nowhere to be found. Jason tried to find the doorway: the small size of the room should have made this an easy task, but when he reached out there was nothing. No door, no wall, nothing but dark, empty space. Stepping carefully so he wouldn't fall on the uneven floor, Jason continued to reach into total nothingness. At any moment he expected to find the door or a wall, but no matter how many steps he took, no matter how far he extended his arm in any direction, he continued to grasp only pitch-black emptiness.

Eventually, Jason lost all sense of time as well as space. All he knew was that the little room had become boundless in size. Fighting back the horror threatening to engulf him, Jason kept walking, his arms outstretched, his fingers continuing to grope for anything solid. But the door and the walls eluded him, just as the window had disappeared. An indeterminate amount of time passed. Then, finally, when least expected, Jason put his hand on the cold handle of the door. He exited the root cellar as quickly as he could, but before doing so, he glanced over his shoulder, noting that the window had reappeared mockingly, its dull square of light dimly illuminating the tiny room. It would be the last glimpse he would ever have of the place. Nothing afterwards could force him to go near the root cellar.

From that day to the present, the house in Harrington has been distinguished by an unusually large amount of spiritual activity. A staff member we'll refer to as Janet has worked at the health facility for a number of years. Approximately twenty individuals known to her personally have had ghostly experiences in the building. An interesting fact is that the sightings occur only where there once was an original structure. This includes the main house and the footprint of the barn, which has since been demolished and replaced with a replica on the same site. "Once you go past the main beam, and into the new addition," states Janet, "there is nothing. Activity is concentrated in the main house and where the barn used to be." Oddly, the basement of the old building is quiet now in terms of ghostly incidents. Perhaps this is because the walls of the old root cellar were removed during the major renovations that have taken place since Jason and his family moved away. If so, the effect of the demolition was to release or spur on psychic activity throughout the rest of the structure.

One rite of passage for new employees at the health facility is to hear that it is haunted. Of course, most people are skeptical until something unexplainable happens to them. Some will never have this experience, however, since ghostly activity doesn't take place during normal business hours. Typically, this is something that happens when the place is quiet and nearly empty.

Over the years, many strange sights and sounds have been seen and heard. A doctor, working alone one weekend, was driven to leave early because of the constant sound of water being turned on and off. As he was leaving, another staff member arrived to drop off mail. He told her what he had heard. A few moments later she was alone in the building, and it started again. She, too, heard water being turned off and on, prompting her to vacate the premises.

On countless occasions, a door located at the top of the stairs near the front desk opens and closes on its own accord. While the door is equipped with a closer, which could account for it the door being shut, this doesn't explain how the door opened in the first place. With the closer engaged, someone has to push hard to open the door. While it now leads to a hallway, the door once opened to an old bedroom, which may have some hidden significance for the ghost who is making its presence known. Also the elevator has a way of working mysteriously. One weekend, Janet stopped by the health center to catch up on some work. No one else was in the building. While she was working in her office, she was startled to hear the lift start. A few minutes later the doors opened, but no one was there. Janet tried not to let this bother her, but when the elevator unexpectedly started again about a half an hour later, she packed her things and headed home.

One individual who works at the health center has seen an apparition. This happened during her first year of employment. Upstairs in the main house, the staff member was startled to see the ghostly figure of a woman dressed in white.

The new barn has also been the setting of poltergeist activity. Along a hallway, there are storage shelves that hold children's toys. One evening, when two of the cleaning staff were alone in the facility, they came upon toys scattered all over the floor, which was not unusual. But after the workers straightened up and were about to exit the hallway, something prompted them to glance over their shoulders. The cleaners gasped in surprise, for the toys were again scattered on the floor. Oddly enough, toys kept for play therapy in the main house have never been disturbed.

Countless incidents have set aside the building in Harrington as among the most haunted locations Down East. We will never know what happened to Jason years ago, but the effect was like crossing the threshold into a different dimension—such was the sudden darkness and the seemingly endless space. The experience afforded him a terrifying glimpse into a world outside of our own realm of understanding. Since ghosts by definition cross dimensions, the story of the root cellar may contain the key that unlocks the many other paranormal experiences that have occurred in this old place.

19

Angels of Death

Among the most fear-inspiring ghost stories from Down East Maine are tales involving angels of death. These spirits haunt local health clinics, nursing homes, and hospitals, appearing just before the death of a patient. It is mind-boggling how many individuals—both health-care workers and patients—have encountered these spirits. Perhaps most disturbing of all is the intention of the angel of death. Don't let the name mislead you; angels can be fallen and, therefore, can be demons. Judge for yourself the motivation or the effect of the angel of death when it makes its dread appearance.

In the seaside village of Milbridge, Maine, there is a nursing home rumored to contain two ghosts who come to collect the dying. When Kelly Howard, a certified nursing assistant, was hired by the facility, she heard the tales of ghostly visitations, but she gave them no credence until she experienced them for herself. The first figure she saw was an apparition of a nurse wearing an old-fashioned uniform and a white cap. Kelly, working the graveyard shift from 11:00 p.m.

to 7:00 a.m., was filling out paperwork at the nurses' station when she suddenly felt like she was being watched. Looking up, she saw in her peripheral vision a white figure, semitranslucent, gliding swiftly past the station. Kelly claims she saw the ghostly nurse several times, as did many of her co-workers. Well known at the facility, the apparition always appears when a patient is about to die.

At the same nursing home there is another spirit who also precedes an imminent death. This spirit, or angel of death, seems to be the exact opposite of the ghostly nurse. He is known as the man in black, and an atmosphere of brooding evil always accompanies him. Unlike the apparition of the nurse, the man in black appears nearly solid, so at first glance he seems to be a real individual and has fooled people on more than one occasion. Kelly first encountered the man late one night when she was working alone. Suddenly overcome by a feeling of pure terror, she glanced up and saw a man in a black suit and a tall black hat flash swiftly, yet soundlessly, past her. Thinking there was an intruder in the facility, Kelly checked the doors, which were locked, and the alarm systems, which were activated. She searched all the rooms and even the closets on the floor, yet there was no sign of the dark apparition. Like the ghostly nurse, the man in black is a forerunner of a death to come. In fewer than twenty-four hours after Kelly saw him, another patient passed away. Kelly still cannot talk about this angel of death without reliving the fear she felt.

Even to the skeptic, there is something unexplainable going on at the Milbridge facility. In addition to the spirits seen there, bells have a way of going off in empty rooms, a seeming impossibility since someone has to physically push a call button to ring the nurses' station. The truly disturbing thing, however, is that a patient always dies within hours of this summons. It first happened to Kelly on a blustery night in November when she and a co-worker heard a bell ringing from an empty room. From the nurses' station, Kelly and her associate could see the door of the room where the bell rang; no one had entered or emerged. Reaching out to open the door, Kelly was shocked to find the knob as cold as ice, "almost to the point of being painful." When Kelly opened the door, she saw that the light was off and the room was empty. In just a few hours, an elderly woman bedridden in the next room passed away. Kelly informed me that this kind of harbinger was quite common at the nursing home, happening on average twice a month during the five years she worked there.

In an eerie fashion, Kelly's experiences are corroborated by Angela Looke, another nursing assistant who quit the same facility years before Kelly was hired. Angela first encountered the apparition of the nurse on an evening already filled with mysterious disturbances. The old, clanking elevator, for example, kept going up and down all night for no apparent reason. When the doors opened, the elevator car was always empty. Then at exactly 3:00 a.m., Angela saw the spirit of a woman in a white uniform, a nursing cap to match, and long, flowing white hair. The apparition appeared to be gliding into the room that contained two terminally ill patients. Two hours after this ghostly visitation, both patients died in their sleep. According to Angela, there is a legend attributing the specter to Annie White, a nurse at the facility who died of an aneurysm to her heart on her way to work. As the legend goes, Annie could not tend to her patients on the night she died, so she haunts the nursing home in order to help others pass on successfully to the spirit world, something she was unable to do.

What precipitated Angela Looke to leave her position, however, was a close encounter with the man in black. She claimed that when she worked at the Milbridge facility, more than one employee and patient had seen this dark and menacing figure stalking the corridors late on nights when a patient was about to die. One evening, Angela stepped into a room and came face-to-face with the man in black. The apparition glared at her and demanded balefully, "What do you think you are doing here?" Frightened and confused, Angela stammered, "Well, I don't know; I guess I'm in the wrong room." She left quickly, but is still haunted by the fear she felt that night. The experience caused her to resign immediately, swearing not to work there again, "not for a million dollars."

While the man in black and the ghostly nurse may be spirits of deceased individuals, like Annie White, there is another explanation, more persuasive and more disturbing. They may be the apparitions of angels, both good and evil. Supporting this argument is the fact these same figures seem to haunt other nursing homes in the region. In Lubec there is a facility that had once been an old boarding home. Mary Hudson, a certified medication assistant, used to work at the nursing home, and she saw the spirit of a ghostly nurse late one night in January. Having just checked on a patient who was failing so fast that she was breathing in a death rattle, Mary went to the nurses' station. There she saw a woman in white at the end of the hall. Thinking she was a patient who had left her bed and who might fall, Mary rushed in the direction of the figure. That's when she noticed that the woman was dressed in an antiquated nurse's uniform: a white dress, a cap, and a white cape. Just as Mary was about to apprehend the figure, it passed through a wall and disappeared. Within hours, the failing patient passed away.

The woman in white is not the only apparition seen at the Lubec nursing home when a patient is at death's door. A man in black has also been witnessed, and on at least one occasion in a particularly bizarre form. He is known as the black-clad bagpiper. Valentino Gareski collected this story for me from a janitor who formerly worked in the place. The janitor mentioned that one patient named James was visited by this spirit in the last week of his life. In Valentino's words, "he would stir from his senselessness and stare before him, pointing, cupping his hands over his ears, and shaking his head violently from what seemed to be an intolerable clamor. He often cried out about seeing a man in black that tormented him with the sound of bagpipes. For hours at a time the 'evil bagpiper' would apparently torment this resident. It was not long, however, before James ceased to hear the bagpiper—or anything at all. Was the relentless musical apparition a messenger of death?"

Tales such as these call into question the nature of spirits known as angels of death. Do these specters assist the dying, or do they actually bring about or somehow speed up the death of patients already ailing? Or do these spirits come to transport souls up to heaven or down to hell? The ghostly nurse and the man in black, appearing as they do in more than one facility just before a patient dies, indicate the presence of another kind of ghost. On reflection, these do not seem to be the spirits of deceased individuals, but rather the apparitions of angels, benevolent or demonic. In either case, the woman in white and the man in black do indeed seem to be reapers, grim or otherwise, coming to harvest souls.

20

The Demon Family

Theories abound concerning the origin and nature of spirits. One traditional interpretation is that ghosts are demons who have taken the shape of the dead, an explanation sometimes attributed to the Bible, which tells us that the dead will not rise until judgment day. The tale that follows builds on the theory that ghosts are actually demons and spins terror in the form of most people's greatest source of safety and security—the family. The story hints at dark forms of possession and undermines our trust in intuition, that innate sense of danger that we rely on even if it surpasses our understanding. Finally, this tale calls into question what is real. As for what lurked in the dark woods of Dennysville on a winter night, I leave for you to decide.

Hannah Dean told me the story of the demon family. It concerns a friend of hers—we'll refer to him as Sam—who woke up from a dead sleep late one night. His intuition told him something was terribly wrong, and he felt compelled to go outside immediately. He had no idea why he must go out, but the feeling was overwhelmingly strong. It was similar to that ominous, premonitory feeling that sometimes alerts us to a house fire or an intruder or a loved one in trouble. These warnings protect us even if we cannot explain them, and the same seemed true for Sam, who didn't understand what was wrong or why he must leave. All he knew was that he had to go outside without delay. Sam dressed hurriedly, then rushed downstairs and let himself out the front door.

Cold moonlight and frigid temperature greeted Sam. Then, as Hannah put it, "he got another strange and unexplained feeling. For some reason, he felt the need to go and sit in his car." Almost as if he were being controlled or manipulated in some supernatural sense, Sam obeyed the impulse. As soon as he was seated in his car, however, he noticed something remarkable. From out of the corner of his eyes, he spotted figures emerging from the forest at the edge of a small meadow in front of him. A moment later, he recognized the shapes as those of his family members. In the bright moonlight, he clearly discerned his whole family stepping out of the dark woods. He saw his father, his mother, and his younger sister. Hannah stresses that, at this point in time, Sam was not frightened; he was simply perplexed. Why would his family be outside in the middle of the night in freezing weather?

Opening his car door, he looked at his family, expecting at any moment an explanation for the strange situation in which he found himself. His family spotted him at once, almost as if they were waiting for him, and they motioned to him, beckoning him with their arms to get out of the car. Still in a state of bewilderment, Sam obeyed their command. Then his family, still at the very edge of the woods, coaxed him to come to them. They didn't rush to him to explain their actions. They didn't call to him or speak a single word.

Silently, they motioned him to join them in the forest for some inexplicable purpose. Their eyes, however, never left his. For a brief interval that seemed like a lifetime, their gaze locked onto Sam's. Their only communication was their arms motioning for him to join them—and to do so without delay.

It was ultimately the wordlessness of his family that signaled to Sam that something was terribly, terribly wrong. While his family was still coaxing him into the woods, Sam turned and ran back to his house—a sudden, cold fear had gripped his entire being. With his heart beating madly, he entered his house and locked the door behind him. Then, turning around to start up the stairs, he received another shock. There, at the top of the stairs, was his father, wondering what was going on. Moments later the panic-stricken Sam discovered that the rest of his family was safe inside the house, where they had been all night. Whatever he saw outside in the moonlight was not his real family, despite their identical appearances.

Reflecting on the eerie incident, Hannah wrote, "What I'm wondering is, what would have happened to Sam if he had gone with his 'family' into the woods? Even if it were a dream, would he have woken up freezing in the woods? Or maybe he wouldn't have woken up at all. Also, it's hard to say if he would have remembered had he not snapped out of it and gotten scared. But I think he is probably better off not knowing what could have been." Hannah went on to mention that for years after the incident Sam never spoke of what happened.

Could Sam have been sleepwalking, or could he have dreamed the entire experience? There are many documented cases of somnambulism, and some are extremely bizarre, such as individuals nearly sleepwalking off hotel balconies or cliffs. In one tragic case, a mother, thinking her room was engulfed in flames and firefighters were outside of the building, threw her baby from the room's window. Certainly, Sam's strange compulsion to leave the house and to sit in his cold car seems like the actions of a sleepwalker. From this perspective, Sam's entire experience can be written off as no more than a nightmare. Or can it?

Sam had no history of somnambulism, and even if he were sleepwalking, there is a dark and disturbing quality to the experience that gives it a supernatural, even demonic, twist. As Hannah pointed out, what would have occurred had Sam awakened in the woods? The confusion and fear would have been a shock to his system and could have scarred him psychologically. Then, of course, he might not have awakened at all, but died of hypothermia.

In another sense, the story of the demon family does not necessarily have to have an interpretation that is either supernatural or somnambulistic: The secret of the tale may reside in a disturbing combination of these two explanations. Considering Sam's experience from this angle, his sleepwalking could have been manipulated by restless spirits bent on his harm. Indeed, his actions seemed like those of an individual in some kind of trance. Until the shock of sudden fear, Sam seemed externally directed, almost like the victim of a diabolical spell. Of course, the story may not involve sleepwalking of any kind; Sam may have been deceived by spirits who had assumed the forms of his family. Questions abound in the story of the demon family, but no matter what our answers may be, we can only join Hannah Dean in wondering what would have happened to Sam had he followed his family into the woods on that frigid winter night.

21

America's Most Famous Ghost

lthough few people have heard of Nelly Butler, her spirit is nonetheless the most famous in America. Butler, who died more than two centuries ago, has been called the nation's first ghost since her series of spectacular appearances took place little more than fifteen years after our country's war of independence. Few other ghosts have received such extensive documentation: sightings of Nelly Butler have been witnessed by at least one hundred people who signed depositions about their experiences. And no other spirit has instigated such a storm of controversy. Accusations of fraud and conspiracy were the least of the charges levied against the household in which the ghost of Nelly appeared. Despite her spiritual, almost Madonna-like demeanor, the specter has been depicted as a demon bent on death and destruction.

The events kicked off in the small Down East community of Sullivan, Maine which lies close to the infamous Black's Woods. For over a century, the story of Nelly Butler has mistakenly been attributed to Machiasport, nearly sixty miles away. The reason for the error is not completely clear, but it has been perpetuated because writers never refer back to the original source. This account of the haunting is from a rare book containing some very dense eighteenth-century scholarship. It was written by Abraham Cummings, a Harvard graduate who was a preacher in the region during the time of the events. Machiasport may have been substituted for Sullivan because Nelly Butler's maiden name was Ellen Hooper and some members of the Hooper family later settled in that area. At any rate, Cummings's account states unequivocally that the "phenomena . . . were witnessed by hundreds, in the town of Sullivan, Maine, in the year 1800." With researcher Dennis Boyd, I have confirmed the location of principal people and places referred to in the original account.

It was clear from the start of the strange events that something momentous was underway. In the winter of 1799, the household of Abner Blaisdel began hearing loud and mysterious knocking noises in their cellar. By January 1800, a voice was heard coming from the cellar, identifying itself as Nelly Butler, a young, married townswoman who had died a few years before, after the delivery of a child. Those people closest in life to Nelly were summoned to converse with the spirit, who convinced them of her authenticity. Soon afterwards, the spirit took the form of a glowing woman in white who spoke on religious subjects to increasingly large groups of people. On the night of August 8 and 9, 1800, she appeared to more than twenty people. They even formed ranks through which the ghost passed back and forth at least five or six times, finally stopping before her former husband, who put his hand through the apparition. In the words of Abigail Abbott, who was present at the event, Captain George Butler was "immersed in her radiance so that he appeared white and shining like the apparition." Nelly's most sensational appearance occurred only a few nights later, when she was seen by nearly fifty people, first in the Blaisdel cellar, then when she led them outside in a procession to the house of a vocal disbeliever named James Millar. All accounts concur that Nelly's spirit radiated light and was dressed in white. Although she usually materialized in a flowing dress, at least once she appeared in her "winding clothes," or shroud, at which time she was holding the form of her dead child. One witness, Mary Gordon, writes that "The glow of the apparition had a constant tremulous motion." Many accounts have the phantom first manifesting itself as a mass of light that quickly grew into the form of the deceased woman. According to Jeremiah Bunker, "The personal shape, when it disappeared, first changed to a substance, without form, and then vanished in a moment where it was: and after a short space, the full personal form appeared again in a moment." The apparition glowed and radiated light even when it appeared outside in the daytime. In the words of Abner Blaisdel, the spirit moved "like a cloud, without ambulatory motion."

Describing the phantom, John Simson states, "The sound of her voice was sometimes hoarse and faint, but for the most part it was clear and free from an impediment, and then it was inimitable, and the most delightful that ever I heard in my life." Sometimes the spirit's voice would change direction, at first heard from ten or twelve feet away, then only inches from one's face. Typically, Nelly preached and sang; for example, once she stated, "I am in heaven, praising God and the Lamb with angels, archangels, cherubim, and seraphim. Glory, glory, glory to God and the Lamb. I am going, I am going, I am going to Christ." Her most famous statement was "Though my body is consumed, and all turned to dust, my soul is as much alive, as before I left the body."

However, when events in the community took a nasty turn with accusations of fraud, witchcraft, and demonism, Nelly's messages grew severe. Once, for instance, she made the pronouncement: "Some of you say that I am not a spirit. Others, that I am an evil spirit. The words which I have spoken unto you have been mis-improved, perverted, and turned into ridicule. But I shall see you all when you will not laugh."

The appearances of Nelly Butler in 1799–1800 were not only well documented, but are also among the most convincing of all ghost accounts. It is difficult to envision how the manifestations could have been contrived through ventriloquism, actors, or other means available at the time. The apparition not only radiated light and glided within a few feet of her audience, but also materialized outside on at least three occasions, during the day as well as the night. When she appeared, though, not everyone present could see her, for Nelly would not let herself be seen by anyone who was too frightened or who asked not to see her. The same was true for the voice of the spirit; everyone could not hear her.

Then there is the documentation of long talks the spirit had with loved ones in which the phantom revealed aspects of her former life known only to Nelly Butler and those closest to her. Finally, the spirit seemed to possess preternatural knowledge, predicting at least one death and reporting on events nearly two hundred miles away.

For many writers concerned with the famous haunting, it is a mystery why the spirit appeared in the Blaisdel home, where Nelly Butler had never lived. They wonder why the ghost did not haunt the house she shared with her husband, George Butler, or the home of David and Joanna Hooper, in which she was born. But the reason is presented plainly enough in the account by Cummings, and it lies in a triangle of love and marriage.

The apparition of Nelly made its appearance to coordinate the marriage of her former husband to one of the daughters of the Blaisdel household. Never was a courtship and marriage so orchestrated by an agent of the invisible world as that of George Butler and Lydia Blaisdel. Because of the spirit's insistence on the betrothal, the Blaisdel family—Lydia in particular—were widely criticized and slandered. Despite the storm of controversy, the specter got its way. On May 28, 1800, George and Lydia were married.

What happened next has cast a dark shadow over the otherwise angelic apparition. On the night after the wedding, the phantom appeared to the newlyweds. To George Butler, the specter said, "Be kind to your wife: for she will not be with you long. She will have but one child and then die." In some of the more lurid legends, the specter rises up like a demon at the marriage altar to curse her former husband with a repetition of history—Nelly herself died shortly after bearing George a child. While accounts like the alter curse are fictional, they do point to the perception of something ominous about the specter: Nelly's dire prophecy came true just four years later, when Lydia died shortly after she bore her first child. In grief and, presumably, horrified by feeling cursed, George placed all of Lydia's clothes and possessions in a rowboat at the mouth of Hog Bay. When the tide started going out, he set fire to the boat, which sailed past the old Blaisdel house, the scene of such a remarkable chain of events. Apparently, the ritual worked because a short time later George married his third wife, Mary Googins, who lived to the ripe old age of eighty-five.

The final mystery lies in the fate of Nelly Butler's ghost. Most accounts have the spirit disappearing abruptly by the end of the summer of 1800, when her appearances had become the most dramatic. The last recorded sighting, however, took place in July 1806. In a field at night, the phantom "appeared glorious," according to one eyewitness; "On her head was the representation of the sun diffusing the luminous, rectilinear rays every way to the ground. Through the rays I saw the personal form and the woman's dress." But does the story really end here? It seems like too much of a coincidence that the series of events took place in one of the most haunted regions of Down East Maine.

For more than a century and a half, Black's Woods, near Sullivan, have been subject to legends that they are haunted by Catherine, the ghost that I described in Chapter One. Like the apparition of Nelly, the specter of Black's Woods appears as a young woman in a flowing dress. Sometimes headless, Catherine is always ready to place a curse of death on any motorist who will not stop to offer her assistance. As unspeakable as it may be, one cannot help wondering if the vengeful Catherine and the angelic Nelly are really the apparition of the same woman.

Lessons for the Gleaning

The tales in this collection offer a broad look at the rich traditions of storytelling involving the paranormal in Down East Maine. Its ghost stories are world class in the sense that for pure supernatural terror they compete with the tales told in any other place. The stories compiled here preserve an important part of the folklore of the region, but they also reveal the extent to which this body of work is exceptional. While ghost stories from coastal Maine have been influenced by the cultures of Native Americans and English settlers, they have also been shaped by the natural landscape, the livelihoods of the people, and the growing isolation of the region since the nineteenth century. These influences have combined to create a potent recipe for ghost stories that truly inspire fear.

In a real sense, these haunting tales lend a fresh perspective on the cultural diversity and regional identity of coastal Maine. The popularity of the supernatural crosses demographic lines as haunting experiences and the passing down of dark legends embrace people of all backgrounds and dispositions. Folklore and oral history are by nature collective and collaborative, not the property of one specific group or individual in the community. Of particular interest is the function that ghostly experiences have in the definition of individual and regional identity. For many residents and visitors alike, the supernatural has become a way of characterizing the region and the experience of life here. Down East Maine is a place apart, one saturated in its own special form of the American gothic. Individuals often rely on this characterization or experience to define themselves, their community, and their natural environment. In contrast to the usual depictions of a culturally uniform Down East, the picture that emerges from the region's ghost stories is multicultural, one that combines the contributions of diverse groups.

Ghost tales from Down East both reflect and call upon notions of right and wrong, justice and inequity. The very nature of a ghost, or restless spirit, often implies a violent, murderous end, or a life darkened by tragedy, physical hardship, and treachery. Peddlers, by way of example, were sometimes victims of their own occupation, the isolation it imposed, and the position it inevitably cast them in as quintessential outsiders. Such circumstances characterize the many ghost tales involving tinkers and traveling salesmen. Racial and ethnic tension between Native Americans and English settlers lies behind the Phantom of the Narrows in Jonesboro, where the apparition of a woman is said to appear on Look's Point during periods of conflict or warfare. Greed and oppression caused the mournful procession of spirits who walk the shores of Big Libby Island, where a villainous patriarch worked his family to death and lured vessels onto the rocks in order to murder the crews and salvage the boats' cargoes.

In terms of gender, the ghost stories from the region are balanced. Both men and women appear as the victims and witnesses of ghosts. And the most horrifying specters themselves are evenly divided between the sexes. The same can be said for economic differences, the rich and the poor are both subject to ghostly manifestations. On a deeper level, however, Down East ghost stories contain a powerful commentary on the material conditions of life. We can see this in the settings of these tales, which reflect a depressed economy and the isolation that ensues—the abandoned canneries, the vast and fathomless forests, and the archetype of the haunted mansion bristling with evil. The common element here is the persistence of the past, especially in its moments of penultimate darkness, those we would want to repress and cover up. Perhaps this is the most radical insight we can gather from these haunting tales—the recognition of the tyranny of history. Surely, the dead live off the living as the past inescapably shapes the course of the present.

Children are overly represented in the ghost stories of the region. This can be seen in the dreadful specter of Dennysville who calls for the life of one woman's child. Then we have an Eastport mansion with the apparition of a young girl who died of disease brought to port by sailors. In the same city, a girl's "imaginary friend" turned out to be the ghost of a child who died with her governess in a carriage accident. The old nursery in one house haunted by an infant was rumored to contain a deathly atmosphere that sickened all who spent too much time in the room. In one particularly ghastly tale, the bones of children were disinterred and mixed with the fill used in the construction of a new house; the spirits of these tormented souls tried to return to the house to smother a young girl living there. What do we make of this focus on children? On one level, it speaks to the hardships of life in the area and the high mortality rates among children in previous centuries. On another level, the appearance of children in these ghost stories contributes to suspense, sympathy, and, ultimately, horror when the small victims morph into vengeful wraiths.

Despite major differences, there is a striking continuity throughout the centuries or even millennia of storytelling and folklore in Down East Maine. For the Native Americans who lived here, terrifying elements lurked in the region. These forces are revealed in the dreaded chenoo, the phantom balls of fire, witches and evil magicians, and cannibalistic ogres who conceal their bloated faces. The underlying point is to call attention to a darkness in the land, the sense of a bad or evil place, as seen, for example, in the original meaning of Machias. Early on, the settlers of European descent concurred with the Native Americans that the demonic had a definite place here, immutable and mysterious, but inseparable from the sheer natural power of the land. Is this the final lesson to be gleaned? Perhaps there really is something about the easternmost point of the Unites States that sets it apart in a supernatural way. Regardless of the reality, it is, to be sure, fertile ground for ghost tales.

ACKNOWLEDGMENTS
AND REFERENCES

ABBREVIATIONS

ML-Marcus LiBrizzi
UMM-University of Maine at Machias

CHAPTER ONE

Pease, Lois. "Catherine's Hill: A Trip through Black's Woods—Is It Haunted?" Downeast Coastal Press. 21 March 1989.

From field collections by ML and UMM student: Kelly Howard, submitted May 2003; Herbert Sady, interview with Debora Newell, 7 March 2005; Dennis Boyd, account from local resident, submitted 26 March 2003; ML, interview with Dale Whitney, August 2001.

CHAPTER TWO

From field collections by ML and UMM students: Crystal Czaja, submitted in Machias, 30 September 2004.

CHAPTER THREE

From field collections by ML and UMM students: Samantha Bunnell, interview with Lacey Bunnell, 27 March 2005; ML, interview with Lacey Bunnell, 28 February 2006.

CHAPTER FIVE

Thompson, Thorton. "Jonesboro's Hilton's [sic] Neck Ghost Yet to Whoop." *Machias Valley News Observer.*
From field collections by ML and UMM students: Audrey Dufour, submitted 30 September 2004; Helen Smith, interview with her mother-in-law, submitted 5 October 2004; Christopher Gray, submitted March 2003.

Louise Watts, interview with Fred Watts, 12 November 1963. Maine Folklife Archives. 419.19-20.

CHAPTER SIX
Campbell, Eileen. "*Going Home*". 24 March 2002. "Jaclyn." February 2001. Unpublished manuscript.

From field collections by ML: Interview with Eileen Campbell, December 2000.

CHAPTER SEVEN
Flynt, Alta. "*A Maine Family's History: Down East Tales III*". Copyright 1997–2004. Revised June 2005. Transcript. Ed. Karen E. Howell. Accessed by Beth Seeley 25 September 2004. http://www.calaisalumni.org/Maine/tales.htm

From field collections by ML and UMM students: Jody Marson, submitted 3 March 2005; ML, interview with Samantha J. Berst, 12 August 2001.

Etta Clark, interview with Octavia Dowling, October 1963, Maine Folklife Archives. 61.012.

CHAPTER EIGHT
"A Haunted Smokehouse." *Bangor Daily Commercial*, 26 January, 1900: 3.

Sabine, Lorenzo, *Moose Island and its Dependencies: Four Years Under Martial Law*. Eastport and Passamaquoddy: A Collection of Historical and Biographical Sketches. Ed. William Henry Kilby. 1888. Eastport, ME: Moose Island, 1982. 175–219.

Varney, George J. *History of Eastport*. Boston: Russell, 1886.

Zimmerman, David. *Coastal Fort: A History of Fort Sullivan*, Eastport, Maine. Eastport, ME: Border Historical Society, 1984.

From field collections by ML and UMM students: David Marino, interview with April Stubbs, 30 September 2004; Tanya Dickey, interview with Frannie (Mitchell) Segien, 28 February 2005; ML, interviews with Janet Toth, 28 October 2005 and 5 May 2006.

CHAPTER NINE
From field collections by ML and UMM students: Mary Hudson, interview with local resident, 15 January 2005; ML, interview with same individual, 15 March 2006.

CHAPTER TEN
"Was It Suicide? Machiasport People Aroused over Death of Miss Welch: A

Belief That the Woman Came to an Untimely End at the Hands of Some Person Unknown." *Bangor Daily Commercial.* 26 January 1900: 3.

"Mrs. Welch's Body Found." *Bangor Daily Commercial.* 23 January 1900: 5.

"Suicide or Accident? No Reasonable Explanation of the Death of Mrs. Welch of Machias." *Bangor Daily News.* 24 January 1900: 2.

"Mystery of Mrs. A. A. Welch in Machiasport." *Bangor Daily News.* 29 January 1900.

From field collections by ML: Interview with Teresa Amuso, 19 March 2006.

CHAPTER ELEVEN
Oldtimer. "Looking Backward." *Machias Valley News Observer.* 12 February 1941.

From field collections by ML and UMM students: Jennie Dickens, submitted in Machias, November 2004; Nathaniel Smith, interview with Steve Wierzbowski, 10 August 2005. Syndell Parks, interview with local resident. 26 January 2007. ML, interview with Steve Wierzbowski, 27 September 2005, interview with Evan Dodge, 27 March 2006, interview with Kenneth Hoffman, 29 March 2001, interviews with Dorward Hall residents, 27 October 2005.

CHAPTER TWELVE
From field collections by ML: Interview with Joanne Albee, 9 May 2001.

CHAPTER THIRTEEN
From field collections by ML and UMM students: Loretta MacLeod, submitted, 8 March 2003.

CHAPTER FOURTEEN
From field collections by ML and UMM students: Jessica Brainerd and Rebecca Colson, interview with Brittany Ray and Ron Smith, 15 July 2003.

CHAPTER FIFTEEN
Ives, Edward D. "Malecite and Passamaquoddy Tales." *Northeast Folklore.* Vol. 6, 1964.

From field collections by ML: Interview with Brian Simpson, 12 August 2001.

Louise Watts, interview with Fred Watts, 12 November 1963. Maine Folklife Archives. 419.09.

CHAPTER SIXTEEN

"Lost in Time: Maine's Abandoned Houses." *Down East* Magazine. November 1993. 60–65.

From field collections by ML and UMM students: Gillian Gaddis, submitted 12 February 2001; ML, interview with Gillian Gaddis and Andrea Padilla, Machias, 12 April 2006.

CHAPTER SEVENTEEN

Bruchac, Joseph and James. *When the Chenoo Howls: Native American Tales of Terror*. New York: Walker, 1998.

Ives, Edward D. "Malecite and Passamaquoddy Tales." *Northeast Folklore*. Vol. 6, 1964.

Leland, Charles. *The Algonquin Legends of New England: Myths and Folk Lore of the Micmac, Passamaquoddy, and Penobscot Tribes*. 1884. Boston: Houghton, 1968.

Etta Clark, interview with M. Angelia Clark, 17 October 1963. Maine Folklife Archives 61.013; interview with Leona Roberts, November 1963. Maine Folklife Archives. 61.014.

Mabel Small, interview with Mrs. Oscar Dunbar, 8 October 1963. Maine Folklife Archives 364.12; interview with Nelson Proctor, 7 October 1963, Maine Folklife Archives. 364.30.

Louise Watts, interview with Fred Watts, 12 November 1963. Maine Folklife Archives. 419.12.

CHAPTER EIGHTEEN

From field collections by ML: Interviews with Greg Williams, 28 October 2005 and 16 March 2006.

CHAPTER NINETEEN

From field collections by ML and UMM students: Kimberly Davis, interview with Angela Looke, 19 February 2005; Valentino Gareski, interview with local resident, 17 March 2003; Kelly Howard, submitted May 2005; Mary Hudson, submitted 7 March 2006.